Change Without Chaos:

A Practical Guide to Decision Management

This book belongs to:

Cover Photographs

The front cover photograph, taken by the author in Prague, Czech Republic, August 24, 2001 in the Palace Lucerma, is of the Kun statue, by the sculptor David Cerny. Permission to use the photograph was granted by the sculptor. Photographs of additional sculptures can be found on Cerny's website davidcerny.cz.

The author's photograph on the back cover, taken October 14, 2001, is by Mia Chambers.

Change Without Chaos:

A Practical Guide to Decision Management

David Lee Woods

**Summmerset
Books**

Change Without Chaos:
A Practical Guide to
Decision Management

David Lee Woods

Editors:
  Phyllis Chambers
  Wade Patterson
  Mary Webb
  Dorothy Frye

First Edition
Copyright © 2003 by David Lee Woods

Published by
Summerset Books
PO Box 2252
Walnut Creek CA 94595

ISBN 0-9715509-1-3 (paper)
Library of Congress Control Number: 2003093887

Printed and bound in the United States of America by DeHart's Printing Services Corporation, Santa Clara, California. The United States Government Style Manual and the Chicago Manual of Style were used as references in the design of the book. The type is set in Antique Olive and New Century Schoolbook.

Contents

Why This Book

Many decisions come out upside down; this book is to help you make your decisions come out right side up. Though this book is written from a business perspective, it applies equally well to all decisions. Whenever a group is managing the decision process, this book can help. Though some of the specific business terminology may not apply, the equivalent terminology can be used by school boards, city councils, religious congregations, civic organizations, social clubs, families, or any group that is making decisions.

We all make decisions, and we influence how others make decisions. All of these decisions start with an idea about doing something different. They all revolve around a problem and what to do about it. The problems can be as simple as a hungry family asking what is for dinner, or as complex as a nation going to war. All of these decisions require answers to some very basic questions. This book covers four big ideas for a systematic practical approach to day-to-day decision management: don't kill good ideas, evaluate new ideas, put good ideas to work, encourage new ideas. Use these principles and the Buck-Passer's Guide to make better decisions and do more with less. Though the book is written in business terms, use the concepts and the Buck-Passer's Guide to keep group discussions on track and to clarify the decision process.

Sounds simple, and it is; it is what we all try to do all the time. These ideas will help us not forget some of these important steps. I think we have all made decisions where we overlooked important things. Some of these decisions may not have turned out as planned and resulted in a life-or-death situation. An example might be, "Not today! I'll have you check the brakes next time the car is serviced." On the other hand, it might have been a business decision to save money by not installing fire sprinklers or using fire-retardant construction materials.

Decisions are made at all levels within organizations where something was overlooked and created a life-or-death situation. Another example might be the custodian who, trying to do a good job, is found dead near the toilet because he mixed bleach with the toilet cleaner. Or, a company is reported defunct and delisted on the stock market because an executive wanted to increase profits and thus manipulated stock values.

We have all asked the simple question, "Shall we go out to dinner and a show?" The final answer to this simple question requires a number of interim decisions. At the very least: Do you feel like going out? What restaurant? What show? Each of these interim decisions can stop the decision process. I call these interim decisions the Go/No-go decision points. Knowing in advance the Go/No-go decision points can keep you from unintentionally going beyond the point of no return. Not only should you know that a Go/No-go point is approaching, but all stakeholders should know when a Go/No-go decision is going to be made.

There are times when if we do not make the Go/No-go decision, it will be made for us. As an all too familiar example, when driving on a long family vacation, we may see a Rest Stop Ahead sign. If we do not ask, "Does anyone have to GO?" we know that as soon as we pass the exit, we will hear from the back seat, "I have to go real bad!" On the freeway as we passed the exit, the Go/No-go decision was made for us, and there is no going back. We need to go to the next rest stop and hope that we do not see the sign "Closed for Repairs."

With clearly identified Go/No-go decision points, all stakeholders can have the opportunity to prevent a decision from unintentionally going beyond the point of no return.

It is also important to recognize any emotional involvement in the decision. We may not want to tell other people about the coming rest stop because we do not want to take the time for a stop. However, that decision could eventually cost us much more time. We need to know if we, or others, have any emotional involvement in the decision that could influence the decision-making process.

It is important to know whether emotions were involved in the decision that got us to where we are now. The concepts used to make good decisions can also be used to find out how decisions were made in the past. When we are driving on a vacation trip, we are in unknown territory, but we do have road maps. Unfortunately, in business and civic affairs, there are no maps that show us where we are or how to get to where we want to be. So just as on a vacation trip, when we realize we are on the wrong road, we may need to go back to where we took the wrong road and try a different road. The time we spent on the wrong road may have been interesting, but that time and money is gone.

Decision management is a critical part of every job, whether we are reevaluating existing conditions or considering new ideas. It can help eliminate unplanned decision outcomes that could result in a life-or-death situation for either people or organizations.

Some decisions are extremely complex and require statistical analysis and computer modeling. However, there are many day-to-day decisions that can be made with the practical and simple four big ideas covered in this book. These techniques can help you decide if a more complex analysis is necessary.

When people learn how and when to make safe decisions, decisions can be made at the lowest possible level within the organization. This book can help you make sure that people make good decisions without your losing control of the decision process. Use the four big ideas in the book to help make time-sensitive decisions so your organization can respond effectively to crises or to changing business situations.

A major part of every job is knowing when to say "yes," "no," or "maybe" in a myriad of Go/No-go situations. Managers do not have to make every decision. They are, however, held accountable for the decisions made by their subordinates. This book will help you avoid saying, "Why didn't you think of that?" or "Why didn't you ask me?"

There are times when you need to allow subordinates a level of authority. There are also times when you must be in control in order to prevent internal conflicts that could disrupt business goals and thus limit the organization's ability to survive in a changing business environment. However, with too much control, organizations can become rigid and inflexible and may be unable to change to meet business needs and thus not survive. Excessive rigidity can also adversely affect the activities of civic or social organizations.

The next section, "Using This Book," covers how you can push decisions to the lowest level in the organization and always be confident that people at that level will make good decisions. They will use the Buck-Passer's Guide (page 55) to make good decisions and to know when to ask for help and how to determine the Go/No-go points in the decision process. Use the decision management techniques in this book to make decisions that will make changes but not create chaos.

Charles Darwin (1809–82) recognized the need to respond to change in his 1859 book *On the Origins of the Species by Natural Selection.* In essence, he said it is not the strongest of the species that survive, nor the most intelligent, but the ones most responsive to change.

Both organisms and organizations must be able to respond to change. Organisms must adapt to a changing physical environment while an organization must adapt to the changing business environment. In order to survive, the organization must manage decisions so that it can be flexible enough to meet changing business needs by maintaining a balance between employee work flexibility and management control.

We all are involved in decisions about our personal lives, our social activities, our civic duties, and our businesses. In each of these areas, this book will help you and those you work with effectively manage decisions at all levels and manage the resulting changes without creating chaos.

Using This Book

Use this action book to improve the decision process. To make this work, people need to learn how to use these ideas. People learn best when, as managers or civic leaders, we consider that adults are self-motivated and have vast experience. Adults are motivated by need and learn best when they participate actively. We all learn by doing; to effectively learn these four big ideas, slowly integrate them into your work or civic process: do not kill good ideas, evaluate new ideas, put good ideas to work, encourage new ideas. Do this by setting aside a few minutes during each staff meeting to cover a small part of the book. The book is divided into sections that include questions and blank pages for notes. As an example, many people do not understand the organizational or civic structure. They may not be sure of the name or title of their boss's boss, or know the civic or social leaders. They may not even know for sure who in their work, civic, or social group is responsible for which activities. People feel safer making suggestions when they know where they fit in and believe that management or civic leaders are interested in new ideas and feedback.

Each person can go through the chapters and identify real problems that interfere with doing his or her job or activity. They can then answer the general question, "What would make my job easier?" and the specific questions in each section. As an example, someone may say that arriving deliveries clutter their way and slow them down. The supervisor might not have known there was a problem but now does and can address the problem.

This book is about how to improve the product and the work environment or the effectiveness of civic and social activities.

The decision process is included in **Chapter 3 – Decide Which Ideas to Use**, where employees can take real problems and work through the process to improve the product or work environment. They can use the process to identify the Go/No-go decision points, when and whom to ask for help. As a result, they solve a real problem.

The book develops the four big ideas in the following chapters:

Chapter 1 – Stop Killing Good Ideas helps you know which ideas can be profitable and should be implemented. It helps you keep good ideas in-house so the profits go to your organization and not to a spin-off company.

Chapter 2 – Change Actions That Kill Ideas helps you develop a staff that can encourage, nurture, and recognize good ideas. It helps you build a great place to work.

Chapter 3 – Decide Which Ideas to Use explains the Buck-Passer's Guide, a tool that helps identify at which organizational level each part of a decision is best handled. It helps you recognize that most decisions have many components. It also helps divide a decision into different areas of concern. This chapter lists many of the questions to be asked before the final Go/No-go decision is made.

Chapter 4 – Use Decision Questions Checklist lists in one convenient place all of the questions in Chapter 3 and explains how these can be used by individuals or by teams.

Chapter 5 – Put New Ideas to Use covers many of the steps needed to effectively integrate a change into the existing organizational environment. It also covers where you are in the process and if you need to go back. Without a continuous supply of new and innovative ideas, the organization may not adjust to the changing business climate.

Chapter 6 – Encourage Employees' Ideas covers many ways that employees can be encouraged to develop and bring forth ways to make the company more profitable and a better place in which to work.

I remember an example where a simple question saved a lot of money. An engineering drawing specified very tight tolerances for an odd-sized hole that was to be drilled in a difficult location. The machinist explained the problem and questioned the specifications. It turned out that the hole was for a wire, and in reality there was wide latitude involved in both its size and location. A simple question to the right person saved the company expensive machine time. This can happen only in business, civic, or social organizations where the people feel comfortable asking questions.

1 - Stop Killing Good Ideas

Business, civic, and social organizations cannot make improvements from ideas that are never implemented. One of the reasons many new ideas are not implemented is that they are killed before they are evaluated.

Many of us have told our bosses about ideas to improve our jobs or improve production. Managers have also told many of us in one way or another, "Your job is to work, not to think!" or "That will not work; we tried it before!" or "Only experts have new ideas!" Many of us have been in meetings where an idea was expressed, and the boss said, "Why would anyone want to do that?" In saying these things, our bosses told us that our new ideas were NO DAMN GOOD! When they told us what they thought about our new ideas, we felt it represented what they thought about us.

Statements such as these demonstrate attitudes that kill new ideas. However, you can make a difference in your organization by stopping idea-killing in your own group. Making negative statements is what Andrew Grove, in his book *High Output Management*, calls negative leverage because it takes little effort to make things a lot worse.[1]

Improvements from new ideas are not possible when ideas are hidden or dead. At work, when our ideas are ignored we may not quit, but when we volunteer in a civic or social activity it is much easier to quit. Eventually a person can just give up trying to help the organization. An employee had been working on a book on management for several years when he took a job with a new company. He offered to let the company publish materials from his forthcoming book in its newsletter if it included his copyright notice. After getting the runaround about the copyright notice, he gave up, and the company never used the material.

Know How Much Perfection Is Enough

There are times when absolute perfection is needed, and there are times when something less is acceptable. Most people who undergo major surgery would not want the surgeon, or anyone else in the operating room, to do less than a perfect job. The next question is what level of perfection would I accept for minor surgery? The answer: once the scalpel cuts, there is no such thing as minor surgery.

---

[1] Grove, Andrew. *High Output Management*. New York: Random House, 1995.

In accident investigation, the concern is whether the procedures, training, facilities, and equipment were adequate or less than adequate. While there are times when most of us do not want to accept anything less than perfection, often a lesser performance level can get the job done acceptably. To commute to work, we do not need the most expensive car. We only need reliable transportation.

As a case in point, I have friends who are very upset if their checkbook does not balance to the penny. They will put off doing almost everything else until they find the error. As for me, if it is only a few dollars off, I have better things to do with my time. (Of course, now that I have my computer write checks, my checkbook always balances.)

▪ Understand "Paralysis by Analysis"

Managers can stop ideas from being used with such remarks as, "We will need further studies," or "The data is incomplete," or "There must be several alternative scenarios." I have seen cartoons on the theme of a couple getting ready to go out, and he waits so long to get ready that they miss the party. This type of situation can also happen on the job where the manager may be the one who spends so much time on details that he or she misses a deadline and the project fails. Every project is different, and managers must weigh the balance between absolute perfection and work that is adequate to get the job done. Just what is adequate to do the job? As an example, if something costs $10.00, then $10.00 is adequate to buy the item.

Having more than $10.00 may be nice but it is not needed to do the job. However, having only $9.00 is less than adequate to do the job.

Determining what is the minimum level adequate to do the job and what is more than needed may save both time and money. The classic example of overkill is swatting a fly with a baseball bat. Throughout the book I use the terms "adequate" and "less than adequate" to describe the point at which something will not work. It is often not easy to describe the point when something goes from adequate to less than adequate, such as when do you throw away a razor. Some things get better as we work on them and others get worse. We need to make sure that everything is adequate but we do not want to spend time or money on overkill.

▪ Worrying About the Details

A friend told me that she and a coworker spent three days looking for a one-cent error in the books. They finally found the error, and their boss was happy. That was a very high cost to pay for accuracy. Is this an extreme case? Possibly, although many managers will accept only absolute perfection because they feel that anything less is mediocrity. Consider the following questions:

√ What performance level is adequate for your job?

√ Do some procedures or practices require people to do more than is necessary?

√ Do some procedures or practices allow people to do jobs that are less than adequate?

√ Do some procedures or practices encourage people to do jobs that are less than adequate?

▪ Set Performance Levels

There are acceptable performance levels between absolute perfection and mediocrity. However, it requires judgment to identify these levels. The performance levels must be based on a balance between costs, benefits, and risks. Many people are unwilling to accept anything less than absolute perfection because they are afraid of a reprimand for allowing "sloppy work" to proceed. Right or wrong, many people feel that certain procedures must be absolute.

I knew a manager who was very proud that his staff always followed procedures exactly as written. He felt this marked him as a superior manager. But when a promotion was announced, he could not understand why it went to someone else. A manager who did not always follow procedures was promoted because he had shown that he knew when a procedure was a guide and did not need to be followed absolutely.

In the following space give examples of procedures that require either too much or too little latitude on how a job is to be done. In addition, give examples of ideas that were killed before they could be evaluated.

Notes:

Transform Commitment to Authority

In many organizations, an unwritten policy says that if you want to get ahead, find out what your boss likes and then support that position. As one employee said, "I am not a yes man. When my boss says 'No,' I also say 'NO!' " Blind commitment to authority can cause a total cessation of both the flow of new ideas and of any risk-taking decisions.

▪ Understand Blind Commitment to Authority

There are many versions of the quotation, "There are three ways to do a job: the right way, the wrong way, and the boss's way." Many people become managers because they like to be in control. I have had managers tell me that they believed their job is to tell people what to do and their subordinates' job is to do what they are told. History reports many military losses where the officer in charge would not listen to a lower ranking officer's concerns about the advisability of a pending action.

Many young people believe that older managers know what they are doing. These younger people are often reluctant to question their managers' decisions because of their blind commitment to these authority figures. Even if they see a fault in a manager's decision, they do not speak up. They feel they themselves must be wrong and unable to completely understand their manager's reasoning. They feel the manager must know something they do not know.

Over a period of time, they learn to keep silent, and as they grow older, they may lose faith in their own judgment. Thus, they follow any leader with a blind commitment. Many organizations are based on a rigid, entrenched bureaucracy where everyone is expected to go by the book and not make decisions on their own.

▪ Understand Problems of Rigid Decision-Making Policies

This by-the-book decision process is prevalent in the military where soldiers are required to yield to the decisions of their superiors. Not only must they yield, but they may be reprimanded for even questioning their superior's judgment. As they go up in rank, they will always have a superior officer in charge. When the day comes where they are in charge, they may realize that they never learned how to make decisions. They fall back on the "if in doubt, go by the book" decision process. However, when the decision is not in the book, they may be in trouble. Many business, civic, and social organizations are much like the military in their decision-making process, and the results sometimes come out the same unfortunate way. Many managers stick to procedures because they fear that uncontrolled employee work flexibility may lead a company down the road from order to chaos and finally to its demise.

We can accurately describe some organizations as blind, rigid, entrenched bureaucracies intent on perpetuating uniform mediocrity. These organizations may be headed toward a slow demise and obsolescence. However, the people in these organizations are comfortable, and they know the procedures; they know how to play the game and they do not want to make any changes. People in these organizations are there because they are comfortable in procedure-run organizations.

▪ Change Rigid Attitudes

The uncontrolled shift from a procedure-run organization toward an organization where employees make decisions can be a perilous undertaking. To prevent chaos there must be a controlled transition from an organization run by a rigid adherence to procedures to an organization where people have decision management responsibility. However, people fear change. They may resist it even if the intent is to help them, and they may fight it all the way if it will have a negative impact on their management style.

Organizations can gain the competitive edge by using the creative talent of their people. Unfortunately, many people feel that they were hired from the neck down and that thinking is the responsibility of the boss. "Just tell me what to do, and I will do it," may be how they think about the job. It may be a difficult task for managers to get an employee to come to work with his head on. Organizations need to be able to employ the total person: body, brains, and feelings. When we have the whole person working, he or she can then start being creative with new ideas about how to improve the job or the product.

It is often difficult for older people who have spent much of their career entrenched in a rigid bureaucracy to accept the need for change. If and when they do accept the inevitable, it may still be difficult for them to accept the actual changes that are vital to keeping an organization profitable. They may feel that they are the senior members of the organization, and experience, especially theirs, counts. Since no one has ever challenged their decisions, and they have heard no objections, they feel they must be right.

Some of these managers will never change. However, some may change when a pending bankruptcy or a significant loss in the marketplace looms. If they can say, "I was at fault" and not "Those incompetent people did it all wrong," there may be some hope. There is a story about a person who was promoted and found three numbered sealed envelopes in his desk. A note said to open each envelope in turn when he made a bad mistake. In the first envelope was a note that said, "Blame it on your predecessor!" In the second envelope, the note said, "Blame it on your subordinates!" Finally, the third note said, "Get three envelopes!" Stand up and be counted. You are responsible.

Several things may work when you are looking for a decision from a bureaucrat to enable you to make a change. Initially, break it to him or her slowly over a period of time. First, present the problem and then later the cost of the problem. Follow up with several ways to fix the problem. Of course, your answer to the problem is among the list (and is the best solution).

It might help to strategize and say something like, "The idea you suggested the other day seems very good; I reworked it a little, and I think you have a good idea here." Sometimes, senior members of the organization are reluctant to "give in" to another person's new ideas because they may feel that they will be viewed by that person as no longer having an adequate grasp of their own specialty. This is particularly true when the person with the suggestion is someone who has a different specialty.

Overcome Fear of Losing Knowledge

I think there is one fear that almost all people have as they get older—fear of losing their mental capabilities. We have all known older people who are suffering from senile dementia, Alzheimer's disease or other related diseases that adversely affect mental capabilities.

It can be disconcerting to older team members when others seem to know so much new jargon that it is almost as if they are speaking a foreign language. This is even more devastating when the new specialists are in a field in which the older team member may have spent most of his or her professional career. This can be a frightening experience for some older people.

There is a saying about getting old, "There are three ways you can tell that you are getting old. First, you start to get gray hair, then you start forgetting things, then—I do not remember the third thing." Unfortunately, many people feel that is true of all "older" people.

However, the truth is that most older people have very good memories, and they are also able to combine their newly acquired knowledge with their many years of practical experience. I know "older" people who learn new programming languages with less trouble than many younger programmers. I have also known "older" people who keep up a schedule of work, recreation, volunteer activities, and travel that many younger people cannot match. Age by itself is not a limiting factor; it is the individual's own ability and energy level that matter.

Part of the reason that the older manager does not know all of the new jargon and latest theories is that the manager has been spending his or her time managing and not doing technical work. Managing is a full-time job. When managers surround themselves with the best people they can find, they can profit from those who bring in the technical details.

One thing that keeps an organization viable is to encourage the experienced senior people to spend time working with younger talent. This can be a rewarding experience for both the older and the younger person. It can also be a good learning experience for the engineers to listen to the technicians. What some engineers do not realize is that the technician may have many years of practical experience as well as a bachelor of science degree in engineering technology.

▪ Understand Limits on the Need for Knowledge

Managers need to know enough of the technical details to be able to make decisions about an activity. In a cooperative decision-making process, the team members with the most knowledge about a specific part of a decision have the most input into that decision. For example, the custodians know which brooms work the best.

Chapter 2 – Change Actions That Kill Ideas covers how your specialized knowledge can be integrated into the decision process and who should approve or disapprove of the final decision.

▪ Understand Coworkers' Need for Information

In today's fast-moving high-tech world, people realize that no one person can be up to date on all facets of the industry. Many work groups hold regular update meetings so that their entire group can know what is new in the field. Team members keep each other informed about what they have just learned and found interesting. It may be a new book or article they have read, something they heard at a conference, or input from a friend or colleague. This information may cover new technical data, something on how people interact, a comment about their product or service, or what the competition is doing.

▪ Keep Management Informed

There is an old saying, "You can lead a horse to water, but you can't make him drink." This is also true about keeping management informed. We can take information to our management, but we cannot make them use it. There is another old saying, "Don't give advice unless asked." Horses cannot tell you when they are thirsty, and managers may not tell us when they need information.

Many people do not say anything when they see a problem because they feel that "it is not my problem." This feeling is reinforced when our suggestions are ignored or even rebuffed. However, people sometimes do tell you when they want your advice and counsel. It is our responsibility to keep ourselves informed so we can help when asked. Open communication is the responsibility of everyone in the work group, both manager and team members. This of course means that management needs to trust others' judgments.

If we do not feel our managers trust our judgment, we can say to ourselves, "He or she doesn't care what I think!" However, if we want to help our manager learn to listen to us, we might say to him or her, "When you have some time, there is something that I think might be of interest to you." This is of course a risk; you may become unpopular if you push too hard, but you can offer. Be willing to take NO for an answer.

√ In your work group, are there easy ways to keep your managers informed about important topics?

In the following space consider some of the ways that the information flow can be improved.

Notes:

Overcome Fear of Losing Control

There is a perception that people on the management ladder must be in control. This is more often true in organizations with an autocratic management style and less likely to be true in organizations where the manager is an equal team member.

In organizations where the ability to develop a team concept prevails, people feel a sense of ownership in their team's output, and leaders are less likely to feel threatened by a perceived loss of control.

▪ Overcome Fear of Losing Technical Skills

One of the problems that often happens in management selection is that the best technical people are promoted to be managers. This is because management may be where people can get higher pay and accolades. In this type of organization, highly skilled and enthusiastic technical people who love what they do may feel the only way to get ahead in the organization is via the management ladder. Even though they may aspire to a management position, they may not be good managers.

In many jobs, the technology changes so rapidly that if you are not actively working in the field you can quickly become unemployable. These highly technical managers may fear that the loss of their technical skill may put them in a difficult situation. They know that if they do not make it in management and they have lost their technical skills (in these highly technical fields this takes only a few years), they may not be able to get another technical job. To eliminate this problem, many organizations have parallel technical/management ladders.

√ Does your organization have parallel technical/management ladders?

√ If not, could this work in your organization?

▪ Share Decision Responsibility

In cooperative, flexible types of organizations, decisions are made by the best-qualified people and not by established rules. Such organizations try to cut the counter-productive values generated by the rules. One of the limitations in traditional organizations is that people further down the ladder tend to consider themselves to be of less value and less creative.

When managers make decisions with their team, team members make sure that the managers have all of the technical information needed. All of the people on the team can feel an ownership in the decisions that their team makes.

√ In your organization, are ideas shared?

√ Are teams used to make important decisions?

√ Are there ways to improve decision sharing?

In the following space consider the questions in this section.

Notes:

▪ Support Decision Processes

There are many things to consider in every decision. Managers making a specific decision may not be aware that they do not have all of the information needed. When every team member knows what is happening on the team, each one can take responsibility for offering suggestions and information. When this happens, there is a higher probability that the decision will be successful.

Many organizations use profit centers, which help people in each small group become aware of how their action (or lack of action) affects profits. However, when there is blind adherence to the concept that every action must show a profit, these short-term profits may have a negative long-term effect. It is impossible to plan for everything, and the lack of a provision for short-term expenditures "because it was not in the budget" can result in a long-term loss.

For example, about a week after joining an organization, I asked for a small expenditure authorization to get some things I needed to do my job, and I was told, "No! You didn't put that in the budget last year." Blind adherence to a budget can stymie an organization. In this case, my manager was serious and did not yield until I pointed out the absurdity of his position.

When everyone feels fiscal responsibility for their actions, budgets can be developed to accommodate unplanned "small change" adjustments.

√ How does your budget stymie you?

√ What can be done and by whom?

Overcome Fear of Losing Money

Some organizations have an elaborate budget procedure in which each manager submits (and defends in writing) a budget proposal. These budget proposals are then rank-ordered by a committee and given a priority number. Those with a high enough priority number are then submitted to management for approval and funding. Of course, if you do not spend your entire allotted budget this year, you will automatically get less next year! The way to play the system is to over-budget in the hopes that you will get enough money after the cuts to do what you feel is necessary.

√ From your perspective, what are the flaws in the budgeting system you use?

√ How do these flaws keep you from performing?

√ How could they be changed?

▪ Limit Fear of Being over Budget

In this type of fiscal system, managers may be reprimanded for being over budget. Under these circumstances, it is very difficult for managers to approve new ideas and spend unbudgeted money even if it may have a long-term positive effect on profits. One time I proposed a new idea to my boss, and I was actually told, "All new ideas must be approved in advance!" He did not seem to understand that you could not budget in advance for specific future ideas.

If all expenditures must be in the budget, then consider a small research and development (R&D) budget for each work group to allow some new ideas to be investigated to the point where they can later be budgeted for further study.

√ How much use does your work group have for R&D?

√ What are some R&D projects your work group should or could do but do not do because they are not in the budget?

▪ Managers Must Show a Profit

Managers who are accountable for making sure that every action shows a profit may also have difficulty approving a new idea. They must be sure that the idea will show a profit somewhere in the future. In order to be able to implement new ideas that may someday show a profit, there must be some latitude to allow a

manager to show a loss. How much profit or loss a
manager may be expected to show when approving a
new idea is covered in **Chapter 3 – Decide Which
Ideas to Use.**

√ Do managers fear making uncomfortable
   decisions because of the budget?

√ How does this affect them?

▪ Cost-Benefit-Risk Analysis

When people on a work team feel that they have a
fiscal responsibility in the decision process, they will
help in the cost, benefit, and risk analysis. There is no
question that if you trust everyone, someday someone
will let you down. In the right work environment,
people want to help their organization grow and
prosper. After all, they do have a vested interest in
keeping their jobs. Managers can take specific actions
within their own work group to build an environment
that fosters new ideas.

√ What are some specific actions that
   management could take in your work group
   that would foster new ideas?

√ Do you know of some good ideas that have
   never been evaluated?

In the following space describe some of the ways the
budget process interferes with how you do your job.

Notes:

Notes:

2 - Change Actions That Kill Ideas

When people are respected and well treated, they will respond positively toward the organization. In many organizations, management feels that people are not just machines. They believe that workers will do an exemplary job if fairly treated.

Rules and regulations were written by people making decisions that seemed appropriate at the time. The organization may have started out with some good, sound, easy-to-read rules or procedures. However, each time there was an infraction of a rule or a question about a procedure, an amendment was written to eliminate any future need to make a decision.

I have heard people talk about procedure manuals that take up an entire bookshelf. It has been said that if you looked long enough, you could find some regulation that would prohibit you from making any decisions. These types of procedure manuals and the management philosophy behind them have a stagnating effect on an organization.

Managers can take decisive—and sometimes drastic—actions to help release the creative talents of people. There is no question that some procedures must be followed exactly. However, there are some written procedures that could best be used as guides.

I was once asked to review and update a procedure manual. My approach was to make it as flexible as possible. What I did not realize was that my boss did his employee evaluations based on how well people followed detailed procedures. He discarded my first draft and did the rewrite himself. He wanted to tighten up all the procedures with virtually no flexibility. I soon learned that he felt it was his job to tell people exactly what to do and they were to do it. There are many routine by-the-book procedures that can obstruct the creative process.

√ Are procedure manuals considered guides or absolute rules?

√ Is it clear which procedures must be followed exactly and which are to be considered as guides?

√ Do the procedure manuals need to be revised?

√ Do old procedures limit your ability to do your job?

√ What specific procedures need to be revised?

√ What could be the effect of changing the procedures?

√ What can be done to improve the situation?

In the following space consider ways to change the procedure manuals so they make it easier for you to do your job.

Notes:

Stop Actions That Kill New Ideas

Comprehensive detailed procedural manuals can have a devastating impact on the creative process.

√ Are you burdened with excessively detailed procedures?

√ Can they be simplified?

√ Who can approve changing the procedure manuals?

There are three different ways that managers can follow procedures.

(1) If the manual does not specifically say "YES" then the answer is "NO." This is a sure killer of new ideas.

(2) If the manual does not specifically say "NO" then the answer may be "YES" if it seems this is the best action. This will help support the development of new ideas.

(3) If the manual says "NO" and if the answer should be "YES," change the manual. This will encourage the development of new ideas.

√ How do managers in your work group handle detailed procedures?

√ Do the procedures limit your ability to improve your job?

√ Are procedures considered guides or absolute rules?

One of the problems with a slow-changing, extensively detailed manual is that it makes it very easy to defend any action because there is no argument if one goes by the book. This may result in unnecessarily time-consuming perfectionism or, at the other extreme, work that is only marginally adequate but by the book.

In the following space consider ways that procedures impede how you do your job.

Notes:

▪ Stop Unnecessary Status Reports

There are many Go/No-go decision points in the process of developing a new idea so that it becomes a final project. When new ideas are in the early developmental stages, requiring comprehensive status reports can distract the proponent from promoting the new idea. Once the creative process is underway, disturbing it can hamstring it.

Let the person or the team members who are involved in the creative process decide when they are ready to give you a status report. Just because the book says a status report is due "every Monday morning" does not justify the need for a comprehensive status report. Accept a brief status report during the first developmental stages. As the idea develops, more comprehensive status reports can be required. In addition, the idea proposals should have built-in Go/No-go decision points that generate status reports that can be reviewed before taking the next step.

√ Do the required status reports generate useful information?

√ Are unnecessary status reports required in your work area?

√ Is there a way you can reduce the number of status reports?

In the following space consider how status reports interfere or help you with your job.

Notes:

▪ **Periodic Go/No-go Decisions**

When an idea is first proposed, it is very difficult to determine whether it will ever be approved for final integration into the organization's operations. The idea proposals may need to be presented as a series of proposals and not as one overall proposal. The first step may be the approval of a proposal for an idea concept. There is an old expression, "Don't beat a dead horse!" No matter how hard you beat it the dead horse is not going anywhere. The same is true of some new ideas. Some new ideas are just never going to work. The new proposal should always have at least two Go/No-go decision points: (1) What specific information will identify that an idea will or will not work? (2) How much time and money will it take to know if an idea is worth further development? In this way, the project can be stopped at specific prearranged checkpoints and thus limit expenditures in both time and money.

The first step is the development of cost decision points designed to keep the research and development costs within reason. The second cost decision point covers the final market price of the product or service or the cost savings. These costs will be refined as the project progresses. Decision points are designed to prevent the development of a product or service that cannot be marketed because of its cost or that will cost more than it saves.

√   What are the specific Go/No-go decision points in your proposal?

In the following space write the specific Go/No-go decision points in your proposal.

Notes:

▪ Do Not Require Certainty of Success

The Go/No-go decision points that are built into a series of step-by-step idea development proposals reduce the need to demand certainty of success. A Go/No-go decision point can be reached by the team when they decide that "this won't work." Alternatively, it may be forced on the team when a competitor markets a better idea for less money, or when the process where the idea was to be used has changed. The developmental Go/No-go decision points can prevent cost overruns and should be built in to the proposal so that they occur before any major investment in time or money is committed.

√ Are you required to have certainty of success before you present an idea?

In the following space, write your understanding of the consequences if your proposal does not work out as it was envisioned.

Notes:

▪ **Do Not Require Immediate Cost Projections**

When an idea concept is first proposed, it is very difficult to project what the final developmental or marketing cost will be. Requiring detailed cost projects can hamper the creative process. It may be possible to reduce the need for premature long-term cost projections.

The first step in fostering creative people is to have a management policy that encourages the development of applicable new ideas that may not be within a reasonable cost range.

> √ Can you present an idea even if it is beyond the cost range of your work group?

In the following space write your understanding of what will happen if you propose an idea that is beyond the scope and cost range of your work group.

Notes:

Promote Actions That Stop the Killing of New Ideas

People tend to propose new ideas when they are comfortable anticipating that they will get a receptive reaction from their bosses. Encourage people to make verbal proposals such as, "I think if we do it this way it might work better. I feel we can develop this idea into a written proposal in a couple of days." This type of verbal proposal has built in both the feasibility and cost Go/No-go decision points.

If the person who has the new idea is excited about it, unless you know that it will not work or you cannot afford the time, go for it. Allow the creative, intuitive employee to maintain control and responsibility for a venture. The cooperation produces both a deeply satisfied employee and a healthier bottom line. When people enjoy their jobs, they work a lot harder.

√ Are you comfortable in presenting new ideas?

▪ Have Fun—Make Money

Even if the proposed new idea does not work (and you may think it will not), the cost of a few days work may well be worth it if it rejuvenates a person's creative processes. When people's creative processes are rejuvenated, they may be able to have a clearer vision of where they and the organization are going. The decision to let a person play with an idea can have some extensive long-term returns for a small short-term investment—returns not only in the monetary realm but also in the growth of how the person feels about himself or herself and about the organization.

When people feel good about themselves, about their jobs, and about the organization, they can experience exciting personal growth. It is also good for the organization because its employees become more productive.

> √ Do you feel good about yourself, your job, and your organization?

▪ Foster an Environment for Personal Growth

Actuarial tables show that many people live only a few years after retirement. This is partly because when some people retire they do not develop activities to fill what was their work time. They then become bored and may have no reason to live, feeling that they have outlived their usefulness. When they stop finding new and interesting things to do they may tend to look backward to the "good old days" and not forward to new activities. Unfortunately, in many organizations, there are also people who come to work every day but are already in retirement. They are caught by the golden handcuffs. They have lost interest in their jobs, and they have been in the system too many years to change jobs. On-the-job retirement is not restricted to older people; many younger people find work boring and they would like to return to the excitement of their youth.

In addition, their self-esteem may have deteriorated to the point where they feel they could never find another job, or that any other job would be just as boring. They continue to do their job but just enough to get by. They just hide out until they are fired, finally retire, or die, whichever comes first. Such employees are in a dreadful personal position and they are a terrible loss to the organization.

On-the-job retirement is not necessary. It is possible for organizations to build an environment where people can be excited about their job until well past the normal age for retirement. Some of these dynamic people continue to consult with their organization long after retirement.

√ Without naming names, do you see some of your coworkers who have taken on-the-job retirement?

√ What can be done to help them feel good about their job?

▪ Foster Personal Growth

There are many people in their nineties who continue to be excited about their productive activities. In a retirement home I visited, I met a pert lady of 103 and many other lively people in their eighties and nineties, including a pair of newlyweds. The newlyweds met at the retirement home.

We can all get re-excited about life. My mother at eighty-four went back to college to start a new career as a writer. We then gave her the new typewriter she had requested for her eighty-fifth birthday. At eighty-eight she was the oldest registered student at the University of Nevada. At ninety-three, she was still working on her writing and stopped only when her eyesight failed. When she died at ninety-seven, she was still interested in learning about new things.

In organizations where people can continue to grow and be excited about their work, both employees and their organization can profit.

There are two elements necessary for organizations to foster the personal growth of all their people. First, there has to be a conscious organizational attitude to encourage personal growth. Second, the individual managers must foster personal growth within each work group. In order to grow and prosper, organizations need to have the best people possible. The best people are those who have the physical, mental, and emotional abilities to do an excellent job and are enthusiastic about doing it.

People like to do a good job because it makes them feel they are worthwhile. In many organizations, the results speak for themselves. Managers can build an environment where people feel they can do their best, and when they do their best, their efforts will be appreciated. Such an environment is one where no one says, "Why should I work hard, nobody gives a damn if I do."

I have a friend who had a boss who kept saying "more, more and more." She has always taken pride in her work and done an excellent job, and this had been documented on her job reviews. She gave more and more, going in earlier and staying later so that she could continue to turn out the high-quality work she demanded of herself. Soon she was being asked to do more than she could possibly do, so she started falling behind on some of the second priority jobs. Then the boss said, "You don't know how to do your job very well." That hurt. All of her extra work and the extra hours had been unappreciated. She felt that she, as a person, was no longer valued by her boss. At that point, she stopped caring about the organization. She just resentfully did what she could, but her heart was not in her work.

This type of management over-pressure for results causes both a personal loss and a loss to the organization. My friend soon found another job and took a financial loss, and the organization also lost the benefit of her many years of experience. Unfortunately, when she left, her boss never understood why, nor why her attitude toward him and the job had changed. However, she doubts that he would even care; his only concern was about today's results regardless of tomorrow's costs.

Management can help people continue to care about their work and their organization. Results are important, but results can be obtained only through people—people who care about their organization.

▪ **Rethink Commitment to Results**

Many managers seem to have lost sight of what their job really is. A manager's job is to get work done through people, not through warm robots. No one questions the need for results that are profitable. Business organizations have a social responsibility to make a profit. Without a profit, they go out of business, and many people lose their jobs.

In America, many organizations are faced with foreign competition with a significantly lower labor cost. Because of this reality, some organizations have gone out of business or at least closed plants in America and invested overseas. However, other organizations have turned to their people for help—not to ask them to take a pay cut but to ask them for help in cutting costs. Many of these organizations have been able to cut their costs and maintain a positive profit margin.

Asking people simply to work harder can have some negative backlash. How much harder can people be expected to work? How many years can a person work a sixteen-hour day six days a week? There is a fatigue factor where productivity goes down. It is also difficult to come up with new ideas when you are physically, mentally, and emotionally exhausted. Fatigue can devastate the creative process.

Harry Truman said, "If you can't stand the heat, get out of the kitchen." Many managers feel that people who cannot stand the work pressure should go somewhere else. Unfortunately, running an organization on this premise causes some very talented people to leave the organization. Dynamic, hardworking people who thrived in an extremely competitive situation have started many organizations. These organizations have promoted people who also liked this type of working situation. The assumption of these managers is that everyone thrives in a competitive environment and that without competition, people will not work hard or produce the best results. I disagree. I feel that many people work best when they are motivated by the excitement of the job, not working against someone else but toward self-set goals.

In the very competitive field of sports, when runners or swimmers look back to see how the competition is doing, they often lose their stride and the race. However, when they run their own race, putting the best they have into the race, the results are better. And, win, lose or draw, they can feel good about the race they did run. I feel the same is true about work; in an organizational environment that prompts personal growth, people will produce better results because they are managing themselves.

√ Do you feel that you have an opportunity for personal growth in your job?

√ What would you like to see changed to help your personal growth?

▪ Promote Self-Management

People can manage themselves quite well. They do it before they come to work in the morning and when they go home at night. In an autocratic organization, managers are expected to tell their employees exactly what to do. The workers are expected to do what they are told, no more and no less. This system may still work in some types of production or manual labor jobs, but in the growing information-based organization, it will not work. Many organizations now believe that the model employee is not one who simply carries out orders correctly but one who takes responsibility and initiative to monitor his or her own work. They also see managers and supervisors as facilitators, teachers, and consultants.

In order for people to be responsible for their own self-management, they must have a work environment that is conducive to self-management. In such an environment, people must be able to know how they are doing. We have to be able to measure our progress, and managers can help. The importance of feedback cannot be overemphasized.

Unfortunately, many managers will say nothing when a job is well done. Yet, when there is an error, they jump all over the person. The only feedback the person gets is negative so they tend to believe that most of what they do is less than adequate and their work may deteriorate.

When managers give positive feedback, people can feel good about their performance, and then they can use any negative feedback to help improve their performance. In sports, the coach praises the big things and points out how to make little changes to improve. The athlete knows that the coach can see his or her performance from a different perspective and is able to point out ways to improve. In the same way, our supervisors can point out things that we can do to improve our performance.

There are some simple steps that managers can take within their own work groups to get people to suggest ways to improve the organization's profits.

√ Do you feel that you are allowed to be self-managed?

√ What can be done to give you a feeling your boss trusts you to be self-managed?

In the following space identify some of the specific steps that the organization takes to encourage you to develop your interests, your personal growth, and be self-managed.

Notes:

Foster New Ideas

Employees will be more likely to make positive suggestions to improve their organization when they feel good about where they work and what they do. People are not looking for a country club where they can goof off; they want to work where they are valued. When someone asks my opinion, I feel that they believe I can make a contribution. When I feel someone believes that I am important to them, I feel good about myself.

In organizations where people feel good about themselves they try to come up with new ways to help the organization grow and prosper. Managers can help people feel good about themselves, which encourages them to create new ideas.

▪ Ask for New Ideas

There is an old saying, "Don't give advice unless asked." Most people have learned from long hard experience in both their personal lives and at work that this is probably a good practice. If managers want people to come up with suggestions on ways to improve the organization's operations, products or services, they must consistently ask for suggestions.

√ Does management ask for your ideas?

√ What can management do to encourage you to express your ideas?

▪ Listen to New Ideas

When people do make suggestions to you, listen to what they have to say. Not all of their suggestions may work; however, all of their suggestions deserve a hearing. Every person comes to the job with a different background. Drawing on their background, they may be able to see a different way of doing something.

√ When you express ideas to management, do you feel that anyone really listens to what you have to say?

▪ Encourage Playing with New Ideas

New ideas take time to develop. Allow enough time in the schedule so that people do not feel excessive pressure both to get their job done and to develop new ideas. It may not be necessary to allow them a lot of time. Allow enough time so that they can see the applicability and costs associated with developing the idea.

√ Do you feel that it is okay to take time to play with a new idea?

√ Is it implied that you can do anything you want with new ideas as long as it does not take time or cost money?

In the following space describe ways your organization encourages you to play with new ideas.

Notes:

Build an Environment for New Ideas

It is the feeling of "I can make a difference" that encourages people to come up with new suggestions. It is that feeling of being important and a part of the group, of belonging, that helps foster new ideas and higher quality work.

▪ Treat People as Team Members

Many people are intimidated when they have Mr. or Ms. Big Shot for a boss. Some managers feel they are better than their subordinates, who are only workers (warm robots). Everyone knows that leaders are a necessary part of every work group. The leader is not intrinsically better but simply has different responsibilities. When people feel they belong to a group, they work together.

√ Do you feel a part of the team?

√ What can be done to help you feel part of the team?

▪ Help People Have Ownership

As people do a job together they can feel that they each have a responsibility for that job and that they have ownership in the final output. They can be part of the collective pride in a job well done. When they have ownership in a project, they feel good about their part of that project, and they can be proud to say, "We developed that new idea."

> √ Do you feel that you have ownership in group ideas?

▪ Budget for New Ideas

Allow time and money for new ideas. Help people develop the Go/No-go decision points in the proposal stages of their new ideas. Let them know that there is time and money in the budget for new idea development.

> √ Is there time allowed for new ideas?

> √ Can you spend time on a new idea without first asking permission?

> √ Is there money for new ideas?

> √ Who controls the money?

One time I proposed an idea that would take a little time for research. I was told, "We don't do research in our department!" I never proposed another idea.

▪ Reward People for New Ideas

Even if a person's new idea does not work out (and most won't), praise them for making the suggestion. When people feel good about trying, they will talk about their idea that did not work. When this happens, someone else may see a way to make it work, then between them they may develop a usable idea.

√ Are people encouraged to suggest and talk about new ideas?

√ Are there any rewards for ideas?

√ Is the reward system fair?

√ Does the reward system keep you from wanting to share your ideas?

In the following space describe how the reward system works in your organization.

Notes:

Have a Great Place to Work

One sure sign of how much people like where they work is when they tell their friends about job openings and encourage them to apply there. Of course, the countersign is when employees tell each other about jobs they have heard about in other organizations. One place where I worked, we had a department picnic; I did not go because I did not feel like going. On Monday morning, I heard that the only people who did go were the people in the front office and those who planned the picnic. That said a lot about how that was NOT a great place to work. (I left the organization shortly thereafter.)

When managers feel good about their jobs, they can also get the members of their work group to feel good. They can develop a work environment where everyone feels, "We work in a great place." This feeling reflects how management feels about their place of employment. You cannot fake enthusiasm.

√ Do you have a great place to work?

√ What can be done to make it a better place to work?

▪ Respect People's Dignity

People treated with respect and honesty will do a much better job. When people feel disrespected and powerless, they tend to be hostile and not do a good job. When people are respected, they feel they are in a place where they can grow as people.

√ Do you feel you are respected?

√ What could management do to make you feel they respect you?

▪ Help People Grow

Encourage people to learn new skills, to become cross-trained so they can do other jobs, to learn more about who they are and what they like. People who are growing look forward to tomorrow. Work can be much more interesting; when work is interesting, people do a better job. Reject the we/they distinctions. One way to help people grow is to reduce the distinction between management and the people in the work groups.

The pervasive feeling that is prevalent in many organizations is either "Yes, sir!" or "Father knows best." In both the autocratic and patriarchal organization, managers tend to have strong we/they feelings toward everyone who is not a manager. When managers feel this way, their feelings show, and people tend to feel disrespected and undervalued. People hesitate to make positive suggestions to those who they feel do not respect and value them. However, they may make some very negative suggestions behind their backs.

√ Do you feel that management wants you to grow professionally on the job?

▪ **Promote from Within**

Managers who respect and value their people tend to see the positive attributes of their subordinates, and those employees who have the necessary qualifications can be promoted. They can either be promoted up the management ladder or up the parallel technical ladder. When a number of people have applied for a single management opening, only one person is going to get the job. However, there can be some problems if some people feel that they are far better qualified than the person promoted. They may try to disrupt the operations in underhanded ways so that the new manger will look bad, and they can say, "I told you so!"

√   Do you feel the best people are promoted from within?

▪ **Encourage Quality and Pride**

When people know they can be rewarded for leadership ability or technical ability, they will take more pride in their work. When they take pride in their work, the quality of their work will also increase. However, if they feel that no one cares, they tend to do just enough to get by. When this happens, everyone loses. Employees lose because they lose respect for themselves, and the organization loses because it does not get high quality work.

Managers can make a difference in how people feel about themselves and about where they work. Positive changes in the workplace take input from the people who work there. It is the managers who must make decisions about which ideas to use and how to implement good ideas to make a better work environment.

    √ Do you feel that quality and pride are encouraged in your work group?

    √ What can be done to improve the situation?

In the following space identify some of ways that management encourages people to take pride in themselves and their work.

Notes:

3 - Decide Which Ideas to Use

Use Buck-Passer's Guide

Although this is written in business terms, the concepts apply equally well to civic, service, and social organizations. In all of these organizations many decisions need to be made before a new idea can be rejected or become a reality. Who makes these decisions will depend on the organizational structure. This chapter will help you determine who is the best person to make each of these decisions.

If you are in a business organization, some of these decisions can be made by your subordinates, some you can make, and some decisions need to be made by someone with more authority in the organization. You and your work group can use the decision tool called the Buck-Passer's Guide to help you manage the decision process. (The Guide is shown on pages 61 and 214.) Use the Guide to help determine what should be considered in a decision and who should make which part of the decision.

The Guide assumes that the greater the potential impact of a decision on the organization, the greater the knowledge and authority needed by the person making the decision. Decisions must be based on

calculated risk and not on luck. Depending upon its
parameters, a decision may be best made by the
technician doing the job, the first line manager,
mid-management, top management, or by an outside
authority. This is determined by wherever the crucial
area of expertise exists.

Those who make decisions must be able to achieve an
optimum balance of cost, benefits, and risks. All
decisions involve some hoped-for gains and are made
with some degree of uncertainty. There are many
factors to consider when making decisions. Some of
these factors include reversibility, recoverability,
impact, cost, benefits, risks, human factors, and
political impact.

The key is to know how to select the decision maker
and some of the factors to consider when making a
decision.

Know When You Should Make a Decision

Whenever you are confronted with a decision, you have
only two choices. You can either face the choice and do
something or sidestep your responsibility and try to
ignore it. If you ignore a decision, essentially you are
deciding not to make a decision. If you feel that you
have enough information to resolve what needs to be
done, you have two more choices, say either YES or
NO.

When you need more information to help you resolve
the situation, make sure that you know which

information is based on fact and which on opinion. Once you have decided to take a specific course of action, make sure it is not prohibited by procedures, policies, laws, or any other regulating factors over which you have no control.

A phone company manager gave the following example of how a simple decision was not as simple as it seemed. The phone company had people working overtime on Saturday, and some of the managers wanted to let them off early. They felt they could do this by having them take only a half-hour lunch and then leave a half hour earlier. Some other managers also wanted their people to be allowed to skip breaks so they could go home one hour earlier.

The manager who told me about this decision problem was not sure about policy. She checked with the company's labor relations department and found that company policy allowed the manager to adjust the one-hour lunch break to a half-hour break. However, state law required at least a ten-minute break in every four-hour work period. The manager then explained the state law on work breaks and let the employees take the ten-minute breaks and the half-hour lunch.

If the proposed change is controlled by procedures or regulations, find out if they can be changed. If so, you should determine who could change the procedure or regulation and whether making the change is worth the hassle.

Stop Little Decisions— Bad Outcomes

The first question is always, "Who should make the decision?" The selection of the decision maker depends on the potential impact of that decision. For example, is it okay for the plumber to turn off the sprinkler valve on the front lawn without permission? That decision depends on whether that specific valve controls the sprinklers that water the lawn or whether it controls the fire sprinklers for the building. If it is the supply valve for lawn-watering sprinklers only, the plumber can reasonably be given the authority to be responsible for turning it off, though he should check with the gardeners. However, if it is the fire sprinkler control valve, the answer is NO. In most communities, even top management cannot make that decision; only the local fire chief can approve turning off a fire sprinkler valve.

Most of the decisions that you make will not have the potential for a serious problem even if they turn out to be wrong. However, some decisions may not be as simple as they first appear.

For example, the simple question, "Can Joe and I go to lunch together now?" does not sound like much of a decision. However, in one case a few years ago when the answer to that question was yes, it created a serious problem. At a meeting of the International Society of Air Safety Investigators, I heard that at one airport the only two meteorologists on the shift went to lunch together. While they were at lunch, a commercial airliner hit a violent wind shear near the end of the runway and nearly crashed. Even though the meteorology desk was unmanned for less than an hour, this might have been a preventable problem for the pilot. If the wind shear had been detected in time, the pilot might have had a chance to avoid it.

Sometimes what would appear to be a simple decision can have serious consequences if the decision is wrong or ill timed. Sometimes even well-planned decisions can have disastrous outcomes. Matthys Levy and Morio Salvadori describe a number of disastrous decision outcomes in their book *Why Buildings Fall Down.*[2]

Since you are responsible for your decisions, right or wrong, it is up to you to make sure that you have all the facts possible to prevent any surprises when you are making choices.

Use Consistent Decision Process

Most decisions involve a number of steps before getting to a simple "yes" or "no." Most major decisions require evaluation of a number of different factors, and each of these factors may require an evaluation of information. When many people are involved in the evaluation, it can be helpful if they all use the same

---

[2] Levy, Matthys and Mario Salvadori. *Why Buildings Fall Down: How Structures Fail.* New York NY: W.W. Norton, 1992.

process to gauge the value of information. With uniformity in the decision process, it is possible to appraise the conclusions reached and determine why some choices are profitable and others are not.

The Buck-Passer's Guide helps work groups achieve uniformity and a high rate of success in the decision management process. Use the Buck-Passer's Guide to improve the better/worse decision ratio.

The Buck-Passer's Guide is a reminder to look at different areas of consideration and to determine at what decision authority management level the information can be obtained. It also helps to determine at what management level the final decision should be made.

Identify Decision Makers

The Buck-Passer's Guide uses five decision-making levels; these represent different levels of responsibility within an organization. In any given organization, there may be additional levels within each of these categories. In small companies, one person may be responsible for several levels. However, even if one person does the job, there are distinct job responsibilities at each level.

Notes:

Buck-Passer's Guide

Decision Authority Levels

Decision Considerations	Technician	Production Manager	Operations Manager	Organization Manager	Outside Authority
1. Problems					
2. Goals					
3. Action Steps					
4. Timeliness					
5. Reversibility					
6. Recoverability					
7. Impact					
8. Costs					
9. Benefits					
10. Risks					
11. Human Factors					
12. Political Factors					

The Guide can help you determine whether you should make the decision, delegate it to another person, or refer it to your boss. It also helps you determine whom to ask for information about a decision. The Guide can be used for all types of decisions—easy or difficult. Two criteria should always be remembered: (1) if in doubt, ask and (2) never surprise your boss.

There are three ways for decisions to turn out: correct, just as planned; as an error, not exactly as planned; or as a big mistake. I like the following definition of these three outcomes: A decision was correct if your boss is happy with the results; a decision was an error if your boss is unhappy with the results; a decision was a BIG MISTAKE if it makes your boss's boss upset with the results.

The Buck-Passer's Guide assumes that the greater the potential effects or perils of a decision for an organization, the greater the knowledge and authority the decision maker needs. Decision makers must be able to achieve the optimum balance of costs, benefits, and risks. They must make their decisions with courage, care, and hope because all decisions involve some degree of uncertainty.

It helps to think about odds; if you do not have good statistical data, even gut feelings about the odds can help. Even deciding whether the odds are low, medium, or high will give you a better insight into how to make the decision. The Buck-Passer's Guide can help you decide if you need additional statistical data.

Decisions or part of a decision can be more efficiently delegated up or down the organizational ladder when everyone uses the same criteria to determine the appropriate decision level. The Buck-Passer's Guide helps determine that level. The Guide uses five decision-making levels, these are determined by job function and not by title.

▪ Technician's Responsibilities

The technicians are those who do hands-on work. Terms like staff, operator, producer, service representative, field engineer, worker, and laborer often fit into this category. Whatever you call these people, they are the ones who are responsible for following procedures and completing tasks. They are the people who actually make or service whatever their work group produces. They are also the people who have first-hand knowledge of what is going on during production or service procedures.

Decisions that involve only the production process of a specific work group may be best made at this level.

√ Which jobs in your work group or department could be considered at the technician level?

√ Who does the work?

In the following space make a short list of these jobs and include some of the names and titles.

Notes:

▪ Production Manager's Responsibilities

The production managers are often called first line management, group leader, supervisor, foreman, or straw boss. In small work groups, they often spend part of the time working in the direct production or service process and the rest of the time taking care of the management of their work group. Whatever they are called, they are the people who are responsible for designating specific production or service procedures and ensuring that work groups follow those procedures.

Decisions that involve the production process or service procedures and do not have an impact on other work groups or on meeting production or service goals are best made at this level.

√ What jobs in your work group or department would be considered at the production manager level?

√ Who is in charge of production?

In the following space make a short list of these jobs with names and titles.

Notes:

▪ Operations Manager's Responsibilities

The operations managers are often called superintendent, department head, division leader, or vice president. They are generally referred to as mid-management. These individuals are responsible for a specific activity, department, or division within an organization. For that specific operation, they designate the goals and objectives and are responsible for guiding their division toward meeting the overall organizational goals and objectives.

Decisions that will involve more than one work group or may have an impact on meeting the goals of a specific operational part of the organization are best made at this level.

√ What jobs in your organization would be considered at the operations manager level?

√ Who is in charge of operations?

In the following space make a short list of these jobs and include names and titles.

Notes:

- ## Organization Manager's Responsibilities

The organization managers are often called managing director, chief executive officer, director, or president. They are often referred to as top management or the "big wheels." These individuals are responsible for designating overall goals and objectives and guiding the organization in specific directions to meet them.

Decisions that may influence the overall organization are best made at this level.

√   Which jobs in your organization would be considered at the organization manager level?

√   Who is in charge of the organization?

In the following space make a short list of these jobs and include the names and titles.

Notes:

▪ Outside Authority's Responsibilities

Many types of outside authorities control what organizations can and cannot do. These outside authorities may include the organization's board of directors, the stockholders, the holding company, organizational associations, labor unions, insurance companies, government agencies (local, national, and international), law enforcement agencies, and politicians. These outside authorities are responsible in one way or another for ensuring that the organization operates within the contract and does not violate any stated or assumed policies or laws. The outside authorities may ensure compliance by auditing or inspecting the organization's operations.

Except for the board of directors, outside authorities generally are not involved in making specific organizational decisions. They are more often involved in interpreting regulations for the organization. However, they may need to be involved once a decision is made. For example, in most communities, the local fire chief must be notified before a building's fire sprinkler system is turned off. If it is a high-risk building, the fire department may have firefighters and equipment stand by during the time the building fire sprinkler system is disconnected for repairs. Similarly, local officials may need to be notified before certain types of hazardous materials are shipped. Even a simple building modification must meet many different imposed regulations, some of which may be in conflict with each other.

> √ Which outside authorities have a controlling interest in how the organization operates?

> √ Do any of these outside authorities directly affect how you do your job?

In the following space make a short list of these outside authorities and how they affect the company or your job.

Notes:

Delineate Decision Criteria

We have all made decisions that produced negative or even disastrous results. Often in retrospect, we could say to ourselves, "Why didn't I think of that?" Why don't we think of everything? Sometimes we overlook a question because there are a lot of things to consider when making a decision. Not all of the Buck-Passer's Guide areas will apply to every decision; however, they may all be worth considering before making a specific decision.

Every decision consideration will not necessarily require the same management decision level. The Guide can help you determine which decision or management level will be the most appropriate as an information source. On the Guide, for each part of a decision, you need to determine whether it should be made here (X) or passed to someone else (?←X→?).

▪ Identify Problems to Be Solved

Buck-Passer's Guide					
	Decision Authority Levels				
Decision Considerations	Technician	Production Manager	Operations Manager	Organization Manager	Outside Authority
1. Problems	X→?	? ←X→?	? ←X→?	? ←X→?	? ←X

It is folly to make changes just to make changes. Decisions should address specific problems that stand in the way of reaching the goals of the organization. It may be nice to change a specific situation, but if changing that situation would not help reach organizational goals, then maybe no change should be made.

Before making a decision, consider what is wrong and whether the decision will fix what is wrong. Even if the fix is cheap, remember the old saying, "If it ain't broke, don't fix it." If it is a big problem, discussing this decision with people higher up the organizational ladder may be appropriate. Good decision management tailors the appropriate decision-making level to the size of the problem.

When trying to identify the actual problem that needs to be solved, consider the following questions:

√ What is wrong that needs to be changed?

√ Will making the change help reach the organization's goals?

√ Is there an identifiable problem that this decision will help solve?

√ Will making this change meet the needs or wants of the people who will use this product or service?

√ What are the identifiable Go/No-go points in this decision process?

√ What are the emotional involvements that could influence this decision?

√   Will this decision create more problems than it solves?

Address the questions in this section and in the following space identify some specific problems that adversely affect how you do your job.

Notes:

- ## Identify Decision Goals

Buck-Passer's Guide					
Decision Authority Levels					
Decision Considerations	Technician	Production Manager	Operations Manager	Organization Manager	Outside Authority
2. Goals	X➔?	? ←X➔?	? ←X➔?	? ←X➔?	? ←X

Many decisions seem to be the right thing to do at the time. However, some of these decisions may be short-term fixes to a long-term problem and may even do more harm than good in the end. Many managers make the easy decision because they do not want to face the tough decision. It is important to identify the specific goals that will be reached by making a decision.

In order for an organization to run effectively and efficiently, it is vital that the goals of each work group fit in to the goals of the department and that the department's goals fit in to the organization's goals. Many organizations are no longer in existence because their people lost sight of the organization's goals. Everyone in the organization needs to understand the business of the organization. Sometimes decisions are based on "I want" and not on "we need." The ego or emotional involvement can cloud the decision-making logical process.

Before making a decision, make sure that the end result embodies the goals of the organization. The more the end result of a decision is off-target from the organization's goals, the higher up the organization's decision ladder it should go for confirmation.

When determining the basic goals of a decision, consider the following questions:

√ Where does the specific decision under consideration fit in to the goals of the work group?

√ Where does it fit in to the goals of the department?

√ Where does it fit in to the goals of the organization?

√ Will making this change meet the needs or wants of the people who will use this product or service?

√ What are the identifiable Go/No-go points in this decision process?

√ What are the emotional involvements that could influence this decision?

In reference to the problems you have identified above, address the questions in this section and in the following space identify the specific decision goals that would help you do your job.

Notes:

▪ Identify Action Steps

Buck-Passer's Guide					
Decision Authority Levels					
Decision Considerations	Technician	Production Manager	Operations Manager	Organization Manager	Outside Authority
3. Action Steps	X→?	? ←X→?	? ←X→?	? ←X→?	? ←X

Before starting a project, it is important to identify all of the major action steps that will be necessary to complete the objectives.

Sometimes there is a lot more to a decision than at first appears. There could be problems with finances, schedules, equipment, procedures, or people. When the implementation or action steps are all considered, it may turn out that making the change may be more work than it is worth. Identifying all of the steps and the problems that each step may entail will help in the decision process. There is no point in creating problems for yourself or for someone else!

It has been said that some people look for problems to fit their solutions. Or, putting it another way, there are people with answers attempting to find the questions that fit.

Before making a decision, make sure you understand exactly how your decision will help solve a specific problem. It is also important to consider how this decision will affect other decisions that are being considered. You may be trying to modify your work area, and the company may have decided to relocate. Determine whether your decision has a negative or positive impact on other concurrent options being considered.

I remember reading of one military base where they rebuilt and modernized a hospital, then promptly closed the base and tore down the building. When determining which specific actions need to be taken to implement a decision, consider the following questions:

√ What are the steps to changing what is wrong and making everything right?

√ How will the action resulting from this decision help meet the goals or solve a specific problem?

√ Are there any potential problems in the timeliness of meeting the goals?

√ Are there any potential problems with the scheduling of the implementation steps?

√ Are there any potential problems with the facilities or equipment?

√ Are there any potential problems with procedures?

√ Are there any potential problems with the people who will implement the decision?

√ Will making this change meet the needs or wants of the people who will use this product or service?

√ What are the identifiable Go/No-go points in this decision process?

√ What are the emotional involvements that could influence this decision?

In reference to the problems you have identified, address the questions in this section and in the following space identify specific action steps needed to implement the decision.

Notes:

▪ **Determine Timeliness of Decisions**

Buck-Passer's Guide					
Decision Authority Levels					
Decision Considerations	Technician	Production Manager	Operations Manager	Organization Manager	Outside Authority
4. Timeliness	X→?	? ←X→?	? ←X→?	? ←X→?	? ←X

There are appropriate and inappropriate times to take almost any action. There is an optimum time for all decisions. As an example, even though cut Christmas trees are free in January, that is not the best time to get one. However, you may be able to get a very good price in January on an artificial Christmas tree that will keep until next year.

The more there is at stake and the more uncertain you are about the timeliness of a decision, the further up the decision ladder it should go.

When determining the timeliness of a decision, consider the following questions:

√ When is the best time to make a specific decision?

√ Has the time passed when it would be prudent to go ahead with a specific decision?

√ Is it too soon to go ahead with a decision?

√ Will making this change meet the needs or wants of the people who will use this product or service?

√ What are the identifiable Go/No-go points in this decision process?

√ What are the emotional involvements that could influence this decision?

In reference to the problems you have identified, address the questions in this section and in the following space identify the importance of timing in making this decision.

Notes:

- ## Reverse Bad Decisions

Buck-Passer's Guide					
Decision Authority Levels					
Decision Considerations	Technician	Production Manager	Operations Manager	Organization Manager	Outside Authority
5. Reversibility	X→?	? ←X→?	? ←X→?	? ←X→?	? ←X

Once started, some processes can be stopped and started over—others cannot. Once the skydiver leaps from the airplane, there is no turning back. In many decisions, there is a decisive moment, a point where we cannot change our minds and start over, a point of no return. When making a decision, it is important to know beforehand when the process will reach that decisive moment. It is also important to recognize how to identify the point of no return before it is too late. Having a predetermined signal of when the final Go/No-go decision will be made may prevent disaster.

The more difficult the decision is to reverse, the higher up the decision ladder the final decision should go.

When determining the reversibility of a decision, consider the following questions:

√ Can I change my decision and start over?

√ Will making this change meet the needs or wants of the people who will use this product or service?

√ What are the identifiable Go/No-go points in this decision process?

√ What are the emotional involvements that could influence this decision?

In reference to the problems you have identified above, address the questions in this section and in the following space identify the specific steps needed to reverse the decision if it does not turn out the way you expect.

Notes:

▪ Recover from Bad Decisions

Buck-Passer's Guide					
Decision Authority Levels					
Decision Considerations	Technician	Production Manager	Operations Manager	Organization Manager	Outside Authority
6. Recoverability	X➔?	? ◄X➔?	? ◄X➔?	? ◄X➔?	? ◄X

There are times a decision needs to be reversed. For example, if the skydiver decides not to jump from the airplane, the only loss would be a little pride and the cost of the flight. However, once the skydiver has left the airplane and neither parachute opens, there is no recovery. What will happen after that is up to the next of kin.

The same thing may be true for some business decisions. Part of the determination about when to make the Go/No-go decision is how much money and effort you can afford to lose. If things start to go bad, it is usually wise not to "put good money after bad." The time already put into a dead project is probably all a loss, even though that expense can be viewed as the cost of learning.

The cost of recovery is how much it is going to cost to put things back the way they were, or at least in acceptable order. Such cost may include time, equipment, jobs, reputation, a lost chance for promotion, and political disfavor.

However, by understanding the recovery process, you may be able to turn a major mistake into a minor error. Conversely, if you do not consider the recovery process, a simple error can become a serious mistake.

Before making a decision, consider the following questions about recoverability:

√ Once the decision is made, is it possible to recover the losses?

√ If I do change my mind, what must be done to minimize the losses?

√ Will making this change meet the needs or wants of the people who will use this product or service?

√ What are the identifiable Go/No-go points in this decision process?

√ What are the emotional involvements that could influence this decision?

The more the recovery will cost, the higher up the decision ladder the final decision should go.

In reference to the problems you have identified above, assume the decision had to be reversed. Consider the questions in this section and in the following space identify the specific steps needed to recover from a decision reversal.

Notes:

▪ **Identify the Impact of Decisions**

Buck-Passer's Guide					
Decision Authority Levels					
Decision Considerations	Technician	Production Manager	Operations Manager	Organization Manager	Outside Authority
7. Impact	X➔?	? ←X➔?	? ←X➔?	? ←X➔?	? ←X

Change is inherent in decisions, and change will have an impact on a number of different people and situations. Almost every change affects both people and profits. Of course, we hope the effect on both will be positive. However, that is not always the case. Even when the change is good for all concerned, many people will be unhappy because they resist change.

Change means that people must learn new ways of doing things. It may even result in some people losing their jobs, maybe even you. There are times when people have been involved in a decision process by means of which they knew they would lose their jobs. It is a tough decision when you know what will be good for the organization may be very bad for you.

When people are upset by a decision, they may be reluctant to implement it, or they may even sabotage the process. In addition, some decisions may have severe political backlash because the political climate was not considered. The political implications of a decision are sometimes hard to identify. The decision may affect many areas of the work force: gender, customs, traditions, cultural and ethical taboos, and religious concerns.

The more severe the impact on people and profits, the higher up the decision ladder the final decision should go.

When evaluating the impact of a decision, consider the following questions:

√ Will the decision affect a few people or many?

√ Who will be affected by this decision?

√ What equipment or facilities will be affected by this decision?

√ What procedures or operations will be affected by this decision?

√ What will be the overall short- and long-term effects?

√ Is there a chance that the positive or negative impact of this decision could be far greater than anticipated?

√ Will making this change meet the needs or wants of the people who will use this product or service?

√ What are the identifiable Go/No-go points in this decision process?

√ What are the emotional involvements that could influence this decision?

Address these questions and in the following space identify the specific impacts the decision would have on people and operations.

Notes:

- ## Identify Short/Long-term Costs of Decisions

Buck-Passer's Guide					
	Decision Authority Levels				
Decision Considerations	Technician	Production Manager	Operations Manager	Organization Manager	Outside Authority
8. Costs	X→?	? ←X→?	? ←X→?	? ←X→?	? ←X

The cost includes all short-range and long-range direct and indirect expenses that will be incurred because of the decision. Cost level authority can be related to account signature authority; as the cost goes up, so does the decision level.

Evaluating the short- and long-term costs is not new. Some form of the expression "penny wise and pound foolish" is common in most languages and cultures. The short-term savings may result in extensive long-term costs in time or money.

I think most of us have used software that had many advertised features but did not work in the version that we bought. Unfortunately, the developer wanted to get the product on the market before the competition. However, if enough things were wrong, we switched to other computer software.

I have a number of boxes of software that I am not using. I have told my colleagues about both good and bad software. The short-term savings of not doing it right the first time may have had a long-term cost of losing customers.

Decisions cost both time and money; when evaluating the cost of a decision, consider the following questions:

√ What will this decision cost in money?

√ What will this decision cost in effort?

√ What will be the short-term costs?

√ What will be the long-term costs?

√ What are the indirect expenses?

√ What are the expenses to other parts of the organization?

√ What are the expenses to those outside of the organization, such as customers?

√ Should the project be reconsidered because of recent changes in the market or in the organization's financial position?

√ Will making this change meet the needs or wants of the people who will use this product or service?

√ What are the identifiable Go/No-go points in this decision process?

√ What are the emotional involvements that could influence this decision?

In reference to the problem you identify, assume that your proposed decision was approved. Consider the questions in this section and in the following space identify the costs that would be involved in implementing your decision. Also identify the accounts that would pay for these costs and who has the authority to approve these expenditures.

Notes:

▪ Identify Projected Benefits of Decisions

Buck-Passer's Guide				
Decision Authority Levels				
Decision Considerations	Technician	Production Manager	Operations Manager	Organization Manager	Outside Authority
9. Benefits	X→?	? ←X→?	? ←X→?	? ←X→?	? ←X

Every decision is made for some hoped-for benefits. However, the benefits may not materialize. Generally, the greater the potential benefit, the less likely we are to get those benefits. In essence, all decisions are a gamble, and there are few certainties.

As the likelihood of receiving a benefit goes down, the caution in making the decision should go up. Many of us have gambled the cost of a postage stamp to mail in our sweepstakes entry for that million-dollar jackpot. We knew that the probability of success was very low so we made the decision to gamble very little money. However, few of us would gamble ten dollars based on the same chance of winning the million-dollar jackpot.

In decisions where the potential benefits could be very high and the likelihood of success is also high, it is important to seek the advice of your boss. You may have overlooked something, and it is never a good idea to surprise your boss—even with good news. If your boss knows the decision is being considered, he or she may be able to use the information to better advantage.

When evaluating the benefits of a decision, consider the following questions:

√ What are the potential benefits of this decision for specific individuals?

√ What are the potential benefits of this decision for specific work groups?

√ What are the potential benefits of this decision for the organization?

√ What are the potential overall short-term benefits?

√ What are the potential overall long-term benefits?

√ What is the likelihood that ALL of the benefits will be realized?

√ What is the likelihood that SOME of the benefits will be realized?

√ What is the likelihood that NONE of the benefits will be realized?

√ What is the likelihood that there will be significant losses from this decision?

√ Will making this change meet the needs or wants of the people who will use this product or service?

√ What are the identifiable Go/No-go points in this decision process?

√ What are the emotional involvements that could influence this decision?

The greater the benefits, the higher up the organizational ladder the decision should be referred.

In reference to the problem you have identified above, assume that your proposed decision was approved. Consider the questions in this section and in the following space identify the benefits to both people and operations. If there are monetary benefits, which accounts would get the credited savings?

Notes:

▪ Identify Potential Decision Risks

Buck-Passer's Guide					
Decision Authority Levels					
Decision Considerations	Technician	Production Manager	Operations Manager	Organization Manager	Outside Authority
10. Risks	X→?	? ←X→?	? ←X→?	? ←X→?	? ←X

Whenever a decision is made, there is a risk that not only will there be no benefits, but there may also be unexpected losses. For example, there are many potential benefits from sponsoring social activities during working hours to celebrate a special occasion. However, if alcoholic beverages are served and an employee going home is involved in a traffic accident while under the influence of alcohol, there could be some significant costs to the organization.

Risks always accompany a new activity or a change in operations. Potential problems include production or service goals being changed before they are reached; tasks taking longer than planned; costs exceeding budget; errors being made in procedures, training, or reports; and people being injured. There is no guarantee that things will not go wrong. Murphy's Law seems to apply when least expected.

The likelihood of a project's failure can sometimes be based on statistical data. However, for many innovative decisions, good statistical data is not available. Without such data, you may have to base your decision judgment about the likelihood of success on a "gut feeling" about the odds.

Odds of very low, low, medium, or high are better than no odds at all. If you are using a "gut feeling" for the odds, you may want to get some advice from your boss, especially if the odds of success are less than very high. Consider that "it is okay to eat your gambling money, but never gamble your eating money." There are many organizations no longer in existence because they gambled their "eating money."

Each risk has an anticipated dollar loss—the greater the risk, the higher the level at which the decision should be made.

When evaluating the risk involved with a decision, consider the following questions:

√ Are the odds for each considered risk low, medium, or high?

√ What are the chances that the results of the decision will be as planned?

√ What are the worst-case situations that could happen as a result of this decision?

√ What is the likelihood that any of the worst-case situations could occur?

√ Will making this change meet the needs or wants of the people who will use this product or service?

√ What are the identifiable Go/No-go points in this decision process?

√ What are the emotional involvements that could influence this decision?

In determining the decision level, it is important to consider the risks involved. The greater the risk the higher up the organizational ladder the decision should go.

In the following space consider the questions in this section.

Notes:

▪ **Determine How Decisions Affect People**

Buck-Passer's Guide					
	Decision Authority Levels				
Decision Considerations	Technician	Production Manager	Operations Manager	Organization Manager	Outside Authority
11. Human Factors	X➔?	? ◆X➔?	? ◆X➔?	? ◆X➔?	? ◆X

Decisions may affect people within the organization, those associated with the organization, or those who are not at all involved with the organization. For example, the decision to reduce the maintenance schedule on equipment could result in the release of toxic materials. These materials could affect employees, customers, and the public. The effect on employees could cause them to be upset and suffer medical problems. The effect on customers could result in their switching to a different supplier. The effect on the public could result in a public outcry that could incur additional costs for the organization.

When evaluating the human factors of a decision, consider the following questions:

√ Will the people involved in implementing this decision be supportive?

√ What could be the effect on people's physical conditions?

√ What could be the effect on people's emotional conditions?

√ What could be the effect on people's financial conditions?

√ Is there a likelihood that customers would be affected?

√ Is there a likelihood that the general public would be affected?

√ Is there a likelihood that people associated with the organization would be affected?

√ Is there any possibility that your boss would be upset?

√ Will making this change meet the needs or wants of the people who will use this product or service?

√ What are the identifiable Go/No-go points in this decision process?

√ What are the emotional involvements that could influence this decision?

In determining the decision level, it is important to consider everyone who would be involved or affected. The greater the effect on people's feelings and work performance, the higher up the organizational ladder the decision should go.

In the following space consider the questions in this section.

Notes:

- ## Identify the Political Ramifications of Decisions

Buck-Passer's Guide					
	Decision Authority Levels				
Decision Considerations	Technician	Production Manager	Operations Manager	Organization Manager	Outside Authority
12. Political Factors	X➔?	? ⬅X➔?	? ⬅X➔?	? ⬅X➔?	? ⬅X

The political implications of a decision are sometimes hard to identify. They could be political problems within the organization, or problems involving local, regional, or national figures. These might include all of the gender, customs, traditions, cultural and ethical taboos, and religious concerns that might be affected by the decision.

Political impact could result from someone's honest endeavors to make things better, or it could result from the scheming of devious individuals. Some decisions appear to have few political implications. However, decisions made by an uninformed or politically naive person could have an adverse effect on the organization. In addition, decisions made by scheming and devious individuals for their own benefit could adversely affect the organization. A good rule to follow is, when in doubt about company politics and political implications, ask your boss.

Whenever a decision could affect a person's power position or the power structure of the organization, ask for advice from your boss. Consider the following questions about the effect the decision could have on the power structure:

√ In what way will it affect someone's power position?

√ In what way will it affect the work group's power position?

√ How will it affect the organization's power position?

√ Will this decision affect an outside organization's power position?

√ Have all of the gender, customs, tradition, cultural and ethical taboos, and religious concerns that may affect the operations been considered?

√ Will making this change meet the needs or wants of the people who will use this product or service?

√ What are the identifiable Go/No-go points in this decision process?

√ What are the emotional involvements that could influence this decision?

In reference to the problems you have identified above, assume that your proposed decision was approved.

Consider the questions in this section and in the following space identify the political factors that could be involved in implementing your decision. Identify specific individuals or groups that could be favorably or adversely affected by implementing this decision.

Notes:

4 – Use Decision Questions Checklist

This chapter is a listing of all of the questions from **Chapter 3 – Decide Which Ideas to Use** starting on page 55; they are listed here in one convenient place for easy reference. In addition, this chapter covers using the Buck-Passer's Guide as a teaching tool and in a team setting.

- ## Identify Problems to Be Solved

  For more information, see page 69.

  √ What is wrong that needs to be changed?

  √ Will making the change help reach the organization's goals?

  √ Is there an identifiable problem that this decision will help solve?

  √ Will making this change meet the needs or wants of the people who will use this product or service?

  √ What are the identifiable Go/No-go points in this decision process?

√ What are the emotional involvements that could influence this decision?

√ Will this decision create more problems than it solves?

▪ Identify Decision Goals

For more information, see page 72.

√ Where does the specific decision under consideration fit in to the goals of the work group?

√ Where does it fit in to the goals of the department?

√ Where does it fit in to the goals of the organization?

√ Will making this change meet the needs or wants of the people who will use this product or service?

√ What are the identifiable Go/No-go points in this decision process?

√ What are the emotional involvements that could influence this decision?

▪ Identify Action Steps

For more information, see page 75.

√ What are the steps to changing what is wrong and making everything right?

√ How will the action resulting from this decision help meet the goals or solve a specific problem?

√ Are there any potential problems in the timeliness of meeting the goals?

√ Are there any potential problems with the scheduling of the implementation steps?

√ Are there any potential problems with the facilities or equipment?

√ Are there any potential problems with procedures?

√ Are there any potential problems with the people who will implement the decision?

√ Will making this change meet the needs or wants of the people who will use this product or service?

√ What are the identifiable Go/No-go points in this decision process?

√ What are the emotional involvements that could influence this decision?

▪ Determine Timeliness of Decisions

For more information, see page 78.

√ When is the best time to make a specific decision?

√ Has the time passed when it would be prudent to go ahead with a specific decision?

√ Is it too soon to go ahead with a decision?

√ Will making this change meet the needs or wants of the people who will use this product or service?

√ What are the identifiable Go/No-go points in this decision process?

√ What are the emotional involvements that could influence this decision?

▪ Reverse Bad Decisions

For more information, see page 80.

√ Can I change my decision and start over?

√ Will making this change meet the needs or wants of the people who will use this product or service?

√ What are the identifiable Go/No-go points in this decision process?

√ What are the emotional involvements that could influence this decision?

▪ Recover from Bad Decisions

For more information, see page 82.

√ Once the decision is made, is it possible to recover the losses?

√ If I do change my mind, what must be done to minimize the losses?

√ Will making this change meet the needs or wants of the people who will use this product or service?

√ What are the identifiable Go/No-go points in this decision process?

√ What are the emotional involvements that could influence this decision?

▪ Identify the Impact of Decisions

For more information, see page 85.

√ Will the decision affect a few people or many?

√ Who will be affected by this decision?

√ What equipment or facilities will be affected by this decision?

√ What procedures or operations will be affected by this decision?

√ What will be the overall short- and long-term effects?

√ Is there a chance that the positive or negative impact of this decision could be far greater than anticipated?

√ Will making this change meet the needs or wants of the people who will use this product or service?

√ What are the identifiable Go/No-go points in this decision process?

√ What are the emotional involvements that could influence this decision?

▪ Identify Short/Long-term Costs of Decisions

For more information, see page 88.

√ What will this decision cost in money?

√ What will this decision cost in effort?

√ What will be the short-term costs?

√ What will be the long-term costs?

√ What are the indirect expenses?

√ What are the expenses to other parts of the organization?

√ What are the expenses to those outside of the organization, such as customers?

√ Should the project be reconsidered because of recent changes in the market or in the organization's financial position?

√ Will making this change meet the needs or wants of the people who will use this product or service?

√ What are the identifiable Go/No-go points in this decision process?

√ What are the emotional involvements that could influence this decision?

▪ Identify Projected Benefits of Decisions

For more information, see page 91.

√ What are the potential benefits of this decision for specific individuals?

√ What are the potential benefits of this decision for specific work groups?

√ What are the potential benefits of this decision for the organization?

√ What are the potential overall short-term benefits?

√ What are the potential overall long-term benefits?

√ What is the likelihood that ALL of the benefits will be realized?

√ What is the likelihood that SOME of the benefits will be realized?

√ What is the likelihood that NONE of the benefits will be realized?

√ What is the likelihood that there will be significant losses from this decision?

√ Will making this change meet the needs or wants of the people who will use this product or service?

√ What are the identifiable Go/No-go points in this decision process?

√ What are the emotional involvements that could influence this decision?

▪ **Identify Potential Decision Risks**

For more information, see page 94.

√   Are the odds for each considered risk low, medium, or high?

√   What are the chances that the results of the decision will be as planned?

√   What are the worst-case situations that could happen as a result of this decision?

√   What is the likelihood that any of the worst-case situations could occur?

√   Will making this change meet the needs or wants of the people who will use this product or service?

√   What are the identifiable Go/No-go points in this decision process?

√   What are the emotional involvements that could influence this decision?

▪ **Determine How Decisions Affect People**

For more information, see page 97.

√   Will the people involved in implementing this decision be supportive?

√ What could be the effect on people's physical conditions?

√ What could be the effect on people's emotional conditions?

√ What could be the effect on people's financial conditions?

√ Is there a likelihood that customers would be affected?

√ Is there a likelihood that the general public would be affected?

√ Is there a likelihood that people associated with the organization would be affected?

√ Is there any possibility that your boss would be upset?

√ Will making this change meet the needs or wants of the people who will use this product or service?

√ What are the identifiable Go/No-go points in this decision process?

√ What are the emotional involvements that could influence this decision?

▪ Identify Political Ramifications of Decision

For more information, see page 100.

√ In what way will it affect someone's power position?

√ In what way will it affect the work group's power position?

√ How will it affect the organization's power position?

√ Will this decision affect an outside organization's power position?

√ Have all of the gender, customs, tradition, cultural and ethical taboos, and religious concerns that may affect the operations been considered?

√ Will making this change meet the needs or wants of the people who will use this product or service?

√ What are the identifiable Go/No-go points in this decision process?

√ What are the emotional involvements that could influence this decision?

Use Buck-Passer's Guide

To use the Buck-Passer's Guide, consider the nature of change and the effects of the decision. The highest level for any of the areas of consideration determines the decision level for that part of the decision.

Buck-Passer's Guide					
	Decision Authority Levels				
Decision Considerations	Technician	Production Manager	Operations Manager	Organization Manager	Outside Authority
1. Problems					
2. Goals					
3. Action Steps					
4. Timeliness					
5. Reversibility					
6. Recoverability					
7. Impact					
8. Costs					
9. Benefits					
10. Risks					
11. Human Factors					
12. Political Factors					

For most decisions, the Buck-Passer's Guide is a quick and almost automatic process. For some decisions, it may be worth your time to write down your thinking in each of the areas covered by the Guide. As you read over your notes, you may see something you had overlooked. Your notes will also help you discuss the decision with others.

None of the listed considerations in the Guide can stand alone. They are all interrelated and must work in concert to optimize the decision process. For example, take a specific decision that cannot be reversed, but in the worst possible case, the negative results will be acceptable. In this case, the reversibility of the action is not as important as one where the negative results could be catastrophic.

Evaluate each area of consideration according to how it stands alone, how it is affected by other considerations, and how it affects the other considerations. If in doubt, ask; asking can be a means of clarification when you are uncertain about some aspects of a decision. However, asking does not mean not making a decision.

▪ Ask for Help on Only Part of a Decision

One of the strong factors in favor of using the Buck-Passer's Guide is that it allows you to easily ask for specific advice. The following are examples of how to use the Buck-Passer's Guide in the decision process.

Identify the Political Ramifications of Decisions

There may be a problem when you go to your boss and say; "Do you think we should '_____'?" Your boss then has to go back over all of the things you may have already thought about. It puts you in a much stronger light when you go to your boss and say; "I think we should '_____,' however, I am not sure about the political ramifications of this decision. Do you see any political problems resulting from this action?" The political implications of a decision are sometimes hard to identify. They include all of the gender, customs, traditions, cultural and ethical taboos, and religious concerns that may be affected by the decision.

This method shows your boss that you can think through various aspects of a decision and that you are able to see where problems may occur.

Identify the Short/Long-term Costs of Decisions

Suppose a person comes to you and wants to make a decision where the cost is beyond his or her signature authority. If you approve, it will be your signature that will go on the dotted line. If that person can show you how each consideration area of the Buck-Passer's Guide has been thought through for acceptability, it will enable you to make the decision more quickly. This does not have to be a long formal presentation; just some notes may be all that is necessary for you to review a person's thinking on the decision. The Buck-Passer's Guide can be a great time-saver for you, the people in your work group, and your boss.

Teach with Buck-Passer's Guide

The Buck-Passer's Guide can also be an excellent teaching tool to help people learn how to make responsible decisions. This can be extremely important when working with creative people who may get emotionally involved in a decision about their pet project. You can use the Buck-Passer's Guide to help them look at all aspects of the decision. When a person has an emotional involvement in the outcome of a decision, it is much better for them to say, "I guess that's not such a good idea," than it is for you to say "NO." You may have known from the beginning that you would say "NO," but people do not like other people vetoing their pet ideas.

The Buck-Passer's Guide is a good "after the fact" teaching tool for understanding what may have been overlooked when a decision did not produce the anticipated results. If it is done right, other people will not feel you are saying "dummy," but rather that you are trying to help them learn how to make responsible decisions. It is also valuable for reviewing how good decisions were made well.

Consider the material in this section and list in the following space some of the ways you would like to see the Buck-Passer's Guide used as a teaching tool.

Notes:

Work Team Decision Management

Use the Buck-Passer's Guide as a team-building tool. When the work group that will be affected by the decision has input in the decision, people in the group are much more cohesive about supporting it. The Guide forces the group to focus on separate parts of a decision. Without making a decision, they can specifically address the sub-questions, "What will be the short-term cost?" and, "What will be the long-term cost?" They may disagree with each other, but the disagreement can be focused on a simple specific area.

They may not agree on the cost, but they may be able to agree that "yes, we can afford it" or "no, we cannot afford to do it." We make these types of Go/No-go decisions all the time. For instance, whenever we look at the outside of a luxurious restaurant, we do a mental "can I afford to eat here?" We make the "go here or go someplace else" decision even if we do not know exactly how much dinner will cost. Perhaps the decision to go someplace else could be based on how you are dressed or how much time your have for dinner.

Many discussions revolve around "yes, we should!" or "no, we shouldn't!" because various people are concerned about different aspects of the decision. The Buck-Passer's Guide can help eliminate this type of time wasting at work group meetings. Using the Guide in a team discussion process helps delay the "yes" or "no" decisions until all of the factors have been considered.

Use the Buck-Passer's Guide to help individual team members learn the basics of making decisions. Many people find it difficult to make a work-related decision. Individuals learning to make decisions can work through the points on the Buck-Passer's Guide one at a time. If problems arise, they can address specific questions. By following the Guide, decision makers can learn to make defensible decisions. Sometimes keeping a team discussion on focus can be difficult. Edward De Bono, in his book *Six Thinking Hats*, offers some techniques that can help a team stay focused.[3]

Consider the material in this section and list in the following space some of the ways you would like to see the Buck-Passer's Guide used as a teaching tool.

Notes:

---

[3] De Bono, Edward. *Six Thinking Hats*. New York: Little, Brown, 1985, 1999.

Notes:

5 - Put New Ideas to Use

Managing creativity and innovation for profit means building teams that can evaluate new ideas and develop those that are useful. One of the goals may be the need to build teams in which members do not become frustrated when working with creative people. When teams need to undo decisions that have been made, these teams may consider the emotional evolution of the previous decision makers. Making the decision to take away a function requires the same steps needed to add a function.

The structure of many production, service, or research teams may pit people who like change against those who prefer order and dislike change. There may also be people on the team who like autocratic control and want to run the team as a "rubber stamp." The Buck-Passer's Guide can help the team work through these situations.

Efficient teams result from good structure and planning. To ensure success, select which people work best together and which people are good at specific jobs, and then develop the sequence that a project will follow.

Identify Team Functions

Many organizations build their special function teams around a matrix organization where all members have both a project and an organizational manager. The project manager often acts primarily as a facilitator to help the team complete its goals.

Once the team reaches its goals, the team can be dissolved, and a new team may take the project through its next step. There may be many steps involved in taking an idea from its first suggestion to the final incorporated modification to the system. Each step has different goals and often requires different types of expertise for the project team.

As the project goes through the sequence of developmental teams, some people may stay with the project from start to finish while others may serve for only a short time on one of the teams. Each team works through a series of Go/No-go decision points. At any of these Go/No-go points, they may stop further development of the project.

▪ Concept Refinement

The first step in developing a suggestion for a change is to refine the new idea into a project proposal that can be evaluated for feasibility. Suggestions for new changes may come up during a discussion of a problem, yet the person who had the original idea may not have the skill or knowledge necessary to develop a project proposal.

At this point, an informal concept refinement team, which may only exist for a few hours, can be assembled to develop the initial project proposal. Who is on the team will depend on the type of idea and the skills of available people. Speed is essential so the team can further formulate the idea before the original idea is lost.

The project can have a built-in Go/No-go decision point to decide whether the idea is worth a feasibility study. For more information, see page 130 of the section on concept identification that covers some questions that the team may need to address.

Merely writing down the ideas may present enough information to show that the idea being considered is not a feasible one. If the project proposal looks promising, it passes the Go/No-go decision point and goes to the next team. If it is a suggestion for a large project, there may be a need for an additional interdisciplinary team to develop a formal project proposal.

▪ Concept Feasibility

The next step may require a much more formalized concept feasibility team. This team may include members from many different departments throughout the organization with representatives from management, health and safety, engineering, budget, human resources, marketing, technical information, facilities, and other interested groups. It could include representatives from any groups that the decision might impact. Some representatives may attend only one meeting, while others may stay with the project until it is finished.

To increase efficiency, a specialist in project evaluation may head the team. Such a person knows which groups would have interest in a specific project and can facilitate subsequent action. If the project is feasible, using Go/No-go decision points may come into play as the new concept goes to the project development team. For more information about the concept feasibility study and for some of the questions that the team may need to consider, see page 131.

▪ Project Development

Large projects need to utilize a rather formal interdisciplinary team which will develop the project to the point where it is ready to be integrated into the overall system. This team develops the concepts and plans how the project will be integrated. It also evaluates the potential impact of such integration. For more information on project development and planning for some of the questions that this team may need to consider, see pages 132 and 150.

▪ System Integration

This team is responsible for integrating the project into the system. It implements the project planning sequence developed by the project development team. This team's Go/No-go decision points are whether or not the project actually works once it is in place. Many apparently good ideas do not work in practice.

If it does not work as expected, the team may decide that this new concept was not a practical approach. If that happens, it is back to assigning a new concept refinement team to write a new project proposal. But to put the project to use, it needs to be integrated into the existing system. For more information on system integration and for some of the questions that the team may need to consider, see page 133.

Consider the material in this section and list in the following space some of the team's various functions in your department.

Notes:

Develop Team Structure

Deciding to develop a team is one thing, but deciding who should be on the team is another. Some people just do not work well on teams whereas others are excellent team members. This section covers some of the interests that creative people have and how to use creative people on a team.

Not all creative people have the same interests, nor do they tend to use their talents in the same way. Although some people are exceptionally creative, others may seldom have a new idea. However, everyone has some level of creativity.

▪ Identify Exceptionally Creative People

Exceptionally creative people seem to have an almost constant flow of new ideas that just pop into their heads. This flow of ideas can be both a blessing and a curse. While the new ideas are fun to play with, they can also be very distracting when one is trying to complete a project.

Having exceptionally creative people on a team can be a source of new and different ways to look at a problem. However, this will work only if they are allowed to talk about extraordinary ideas. Once started, they may have a torrent of ideas, some of which may seem wild and unreal. By mere definition of the word "exceptional," exceptionally creative people are rare and you may not have to concern yourself with this problem. However, it is possible you will have some exceptionally creative people in your work group and not know it. See **Chapter 6 – Encourage Employees' Ideas** for ways to work with creative people.

▪ Identify Creative and Practical People

People who are both creative and practical make excellent team members because they can come up with many new ideas, but they like their ideas to be practical. They often like to find approaches to doing things in a new and better way. Where exceptionally creative people may want to change something just for the fun of it, people who are both creative and practical want the ideas to be an obvious improvement. Creative and practical people can do an excellent job of integrating a new project into the system. They may be able to solve some of the problems that will come up during system modifications.

▪ Identify Creative and Productive People

People who enjoy finding ways to make the existing system work better are important members of the work group. They want to improve productivity by making the many small changes that encourage the system to work better. Their ideas improve the efficiency of the system and thus the organization's profits. These people need to be utilized in order to encourage their suggestions.

Utilizing the talents of creative and productive people can help you realize organizational profits. Their contribution is an increase in operational efficiency and the resulting decrease in costs.

Consider the material in this section and list in the following space some of the different team structures in your department.

Notes:

Use Multi-Level
Project Proposals

Many organizational changes are small changes that improve how something is done. A change may decrease the time required to complete a procedure and could be as simple as moving the supplies closer to the workstation. Although this may save only a few minutes each trip, if many people save a few minutes many times a day, that can be a real savings in time, and time is money. There may be a simple way to reduce the amount of scrap generated by a process or to reduce the risk of an injury or equipment damage.

Reducing the purchasing cost of items may also save money. However, low-bid items are not necessarily money savers. For example, consider a situation where a very expensive item was subject to a great deal of accidental damage during production. The item was cylindrical, about eight inches in diameter, and weighed approximately twenty pounds. It was moved among many workstations on a cart. The problem was that the item frequently rolled off the cart or workbench. The organization had a strict low-bid purchasing policy; following the policy, they purchased the standard type of audiovisual equipment cart to move the items from one workstation to the next. Building a special cart solved the problem. It held the item throughout the production steps so there was no more damage due to dropping. The low-bid carts were an expensive way to attempt to save money. Even though custom-built carts were more expensive, they paid for themselves by reducing the losses during the production steps.

Some very simple changes can save a lot of money. Other changes are much more complex and may require many steps during development before the change can be accomplished. All these changes take planning. The amount of planning will depend on the magnitude of the change. Many poor decisions result from too much planning. By contrast, from management ego, there may be the temptation to say, "I don't need a plan; I'm sure I can handle whatever develops."

When a proposed change will require more than a simple modification, there are a number of steps that should be considered during the planning stage. The larger the project, the more planning will be required during each of these steps.

The purpose of a multi-level project proposal is to reduce the likelihood that a project can get out of hand. By dividing the project development into several distinct phases, it is much easier to incorporate a series of Go/No-go decision points.

▪ Concept Identification

The first step in a simple change is often no more than a discussion. For a more complex idea of a proposed change, it may be advisable to develop a written proposal. The first Go/No-go decision point past oral approval is the development of a written description of the general problem and the projected goals.

The second Go/No-go decision point identifies specific problems that may be encountered while meeting defined goals.

√ Is solving the problems worth the cost and effort to take the next step?

▪ Concept Feasibility Study

After the basic concept has been approved, it is necessary to determine whether it is reasonable to implement the proposed change. This phase identifies the decision considerations covered in the Buck-Passer's Guide in **Chapter 3 – Decide Which Ideas to Use**.

Each of these concerns is listed below by title only, with additional information and questions included in the section "Delineate Decision Criteria."

√ Identify problems to be solved

√ Identify decision goals

√ Identify action steps

√ Determine timeliness of decisions

√ Reverse bad decisions

√ Recover from bad decisions

√ Identify the impact of decisions

√ Identify short/long-term costs of decisions

√ Identify projected benefits of decisions

√ Identify potential decision risks

√ Determine how decisions affect people

√ Identify the political ramifications of decisions

In addition to the above considerations, there are practical considerations covered later in Chapter 5 under project sequence.

▪ Project Development

Even after the project has been developed and is ready for integration into normal operations, it may not be appropriate to integrate it. To pass the last Go/No-go decision point, the following considerations may also need to be evaluated:

√ Has the reason for doing this project changed?

√ Has the market changed since the project was started?

√ Is the project still financially viable?

√ Has the process or activity that is to use this project changed?

√ Has the organization changed since the
project was started?

▪ System Integration

A number of questions need to be considered before
integrating a project. During this phase, it is
important to reevaluate how the decision
considerations listed above will be impacted by the
integration of the project.

Even though a great deal of time, money, and ego have
gone into this project, reconsider the reasonableness of
implementing the project.

Consider the material and questions in this section
and list in the following space some things that need to
be addressed in your project proposal.

Notes:

Project Sequence

People do not like to be shown they are wrong, especially if the mistake is an obvious oversight. None of us likes that dumb feeling that goes with "why didn't I think of that?" To avoid such humiliation, consider the logical order in which various decision considerations occur. Not all projects will fit the pattern listed in this section. What will be needed is for each of these considerations to be reevaluated at each step of the project conception and development. Every one of these considerations must be evaluated as a Go/No-go decision point at each stage of the project development.

These considerations are listed below by title, and additional questions in each of these areas are covered later.

√ Identify organizational goals

√ Identify written and unwritten policies

√ Identify approval authority

√ Identify financial responsibility

√ Define scheduling needs

√ Define facilities and equipment requirements

√ Define procedures and training needs

√   Define human resources needs

Each of these decision considerations should be addressed. The extent of the proposal will be determined by the complexity of the proposed change and how much the change will interact with other processes. Each of these considerations can be a Go/No-go decision point. If the proposal passes all of the Go/No-go decision points in this phase, it is ready for the project development Go/No-go decision.

▪ Identify Project Considerations

Addressing each of these sequence considerations is part of planning a project proposal. Not evaluating each of these points could result in a costly but preventable oversight and the ensuing "dumb" syndrome. Unfortunately, many of us have learned this lesson the hard way, and we, it is hoped, have learned things we will not forget next time.

Identify Organizational Goals

The most brilliant new idea may not be suitable for a specific organization. The new idea must fit into the business of the organization. A concept for a new electronic device is not of much value to a firm that makes furniture. The new idea must fit into the overall written and unwritten goals of the organization. The organization that has been established in a community for many years has a different community service goal than the fly-by-night organization that may be around only long enough to make a big profit and then move on.

In the following space evaluate the match between the proposed new idea and the organizational goals.

Notes:

Identify Written and Unwritten Policies

The organization's policies are (ideally) a written reflection of the organization's goals. In addition, there are unwritten policies that management also uses in the decision process. Some of these unwritten policies are obvious and some are not, and more important, some are in direct conflict with the written policies. The organization may have a written and well-published policy of having a safe working place for all employees. However, the unwritten and not published policy may be to spend little time or money on the safety program. This contradiction could result in a proposal for a change to make an operation safer, which is in keeping with the written policy. The proposal may well get a lot of talk about approval and maybe even some time for a committee to study it further. However, in the end, it may not get funded and will die.

When looking over the organization's policies and procedures manuals, it may well be worth considering whether they are themselves current and usable. Written policies have a tendency to just keep on growing; seldom are they cut back.

All proposed new ideas should be compatible with the unwritten, written, and/or rewritten policies. If the policies stand in the way of reaching the organization's goals, they may be outdated and need to be replaced.

Identify Approval Authority

Before a project can be approved, someone must take the responsibility to make the Go/No-go decision. This person's signature must approve the time and money needed at each specific stage of a project.

The new idea proposal must identify the approval authority for the project. **Chapter 3 – Decide Which Ideas to Use** covers how to identify who should make the proposal approval decision.

Identify Financial Responsibility

If something is going to be done, someone is going to have to pay for it with both the time and the actual expenditure of funds. This may seem obvious, but it is not always. I once was assigned to develop an emergency response training program that would eventually involve a large expenditure of time from people in a different department. I had worked closely with two department heads during the development of the project and both men seemed pleased with the results. All was well until it was time to charge the workers' time to an account number.

At that point both managers said, "Their time does not get charged to my account number!" The project then died a sudden death, and that oversight showed up on my annual review. I had not made sure who was going to take financial responsibility for the project. Be sure that financial responsibility is included in the list of considerations and that the person with signature authority for each account approves it in advance.

Make sure the proposal includes, in writing, who has financial responsibility and which account numbers will be used for both the time and expenditures. Make sure that the funding source for each activity has been identified and that the budget limits have been established for capital, operations, and payroll expenses. It may also be important to identify how the accounting will be handled.

Define Scheduling Needs

The first consideration is to define how activities will be scheduled. As the project goes from conception to final integration into the system, the scheduling may become more complex. Schedules include both the design and use of a scheduling system that will give reports on when each activity is to start, the elapsed time, schedule slack time, and the critical scheduling points that could affect the meeting of project goals. The system may vary in complexity from notes on a whiteboard to a computer-assisted, critical-path management system.

In setting up a scheduling system, there are a number of questions that need to be addressed.

√ How much time will it take to do each activity?

√ When will each activity be started and finished?

√ Has the type of information the scheduling system can report been identified?

√ Has the type of scheduling system that will be used been identified?

√ Have the equipment, fiscal, and personnel requirements for the scheduling system been delineated?

Make sure that the scheduling procedures are included in the new idea proposal.

Define Facilities and Equipment Requirements

Every new project needs a location and some equipment with which to perform the tasks. The project may be developed, using existing facilities and equipment, concurrent with other normal activities. However, if the existing facilities and equipment are being used to the maximum, there may not be any way to fit in the new project.

The facilities and equipment include all the physical things needed such as land, site development, buildings, facilities, equipment, vehicles, office furniture, supplies, etc. Before approving a project, there are a number of considerations about the facilities and equipment that must be delineated.

√ Where will each activity be done?

√ What will be needed to do each activity?

√ Has all of the equipment needed to meet each activity goal been identified?

√ Is it likely people will be required to exceed their capabilities when they are designing, building, installing, using, maintaining, and disposing of materials and equipment?

√ Will materials or any piece of equipment exceed the electrical, mechanical, or chemical limits of other materials or equipment with which it will interact?

√ Have all of the requirements of outside authorities been met, including laws, codes, standards, and special requirements of governing boards, etc.?

When delineating the facilities and equipment needs of a new project under consideration, it is important to make sure that everything is included within the proposed and approved budget.

Define Procedures and Training Needs

In order to do any project, people need to know what they are supposed to do and how to do it. This may require some new written or unwritten procedures. It may also require some formal or informal training. It may be necessary to review both the existing and proposed procedures, manuals, technical training, and interpersonal development. There are a number of questions that may need to be addressed.

√ What do the personnel involved need to know, learn, or find out?

√ Have the procedures and training needed to safely and efficiently meet each activity goal been identified?

√ Do the procedures and training cover all the activities needed during normal operation?

√ Do the procedures and training include emergency preparedness procedures?

√ Do the procedures and training address all of the gender, customs, tradition, cultural and ethical taboos, and religious concerns that may affect the employees?

Define Human Resource Needs

Human resources include all of the direct and indirect support that will be involved in both normal operations and emergency preparedness activities.

Personnel needs include specific talents; number of people; when and how long people will be on the staff; what training will be given before, during and after the project; organizational structure; policies to be followed; housing requirements; salary structure; and position classification. There are a number of questions about personnel needs that need to be considered.

√ Are specific roles assigned to identifiable personnel?

√ Have the personnel needs of each activity been identified?

√ Are the people who are to implement the project available?

√ Does the personnel selection process address all of the gender, customs, tradition, cultural and ethical taboos, and religious concerns that may affect the employees?

Consider the material and questions in this section and list in the following space some things that need to be addressed in your project proposal.

Notes:

▪ Delineate Concept Identification

Behind any proposal, there are some basic concepts. Identifying these concepts helps to determine whether the proposal will be helpful to the organization.

Identify Problem

A good way to start is to clearly identify what is wrong with the existing system. Problem identification answers the question, "What is wrong as things are NOW?" If a problem is projected to occur, then the NOW involves the necessary preparation to handle the projected problem. We know we will have earthquakes, but we are not having one NOW. However, that does not mean that earthquake preparedness is not a NOW problem. For more specifics, see the Buck-Passer's Guide in **Chapter 3 – Decide Which Ideas to Use**, and the section "Identify Problems to Be Solved."

Even though all problems cannot be solved and all goals cannot be reached, it does help to know what is wrong and what might be done to change things. You may be trying to solve the wrong problem unless the problem is written down and agreed upon before any other steps are taken.

Clarify Goals

Goals clarification answers the question, "How would I like things to be?" Sometimes just clarifying the goals makes one see that they are reachable. The goals become more clear when one realizes that the end result will be more effective than the way things are now. Like the problem, the goals need to be written and agreed upon so that you end up with what you really want. For more information, see the Buck-Passer's Guide in **Chapter 3 – Decide Which Ideas to Use**, and the section "Identify Decision Goals."

Notes:

Specify Project Objective

Objective specification answers the question, "If you don't like it, what are you going to do about it?" Identify each of the steps that are necessary to go from how things are now to where things could be. These are the objectives of the project that must be specified. Only when steps are specified can they be evaluated. Even though the problem is real and the goal laudable, some of the steps necessary to fix the problem may not be possible. All of the objectives must be realistic and feasible.

Conduct Feasibility Study

Feasibility assesses whether the objective can actually be accomplished, and if it can, whether it is economically reasonable to try and accomplish it. I may set a goal of becoming an excellent runner, but one of the objectives along the way is to get into competitive physical condition. Considering my athletic ability and my age, that may not be a feasible objective to accomplish. On the other hand, a young person who is a good athlete may also have the same goal and be able to achieve that objective, yet not have enough money to make it feasible. Considering whether this is the best place to spend time and money is a critical part of the decision process. If time and money is spent on one project, it cannot be spent on some other one.

    √ Which project involves the best use of time and money?

√ In the future, will there be an opportune time for this project?

Evaluate Scheduling Considerations

Time is always a problem; by the time the project can be finished, it may not be needed. Many things can keep a project from being completed on time. For example, if you need a new roof, it is best to do it before it rains. Even though you want a new roof, the roofing contractors may already have a full schedule. Everything that will influence scheduling the work needed to complete the objective must be identified in order to accommodate the proposed schedule. For more information, see the Buck-Passer's Guide in **Chapter 3 – Decide Which Ideas to Use**, and the section "Determine Timeliness of Decisions."

Notes:

Do Feasibility Study

Even if there is a problem and reasonable goals with do-able objectives, it may not be a good decision to develop and implement the proposed project. For example, adding additional safety guards may make a piece of equipment absolutely safe, but if that equipment will be phased out before the guards can be installed, it does not make much sense to start the project.

Evaluate Proposal's Applicability

Before starting a proposed project, consider whether it can be done and should be done. Is the proposed project in the area in which your organization has expertise? Consider whether the moral, cultural, and ecological impact of the proposal may create additional hidden costs that may outweigh the short-term benefits.

Estimate Development Costs

Identify all the costs necessary to develop this proposal through each of the development stages. Then, consider whether it is a good financial risk. Being able to afford something does not necessarily justify buying it.

Evaluate Marketing Considerations

Consider the information from the market analysis and whether it indicates that the end product or service will sell at a profit. No matter how good it seems to be, do not make it if you cannot sell it. Alternatively, in the civic world the market is public use of a facility. The "market" or public use must be justified by how well a proposed project meets the public need. There are many seldom-used named facilities which stand primarily as a monument to someone's term in public office. In many cases, a great deal of public money was spent on a facility that met an ego need but not the public need.

Consider the material and questions in this section and list in the following space the major steps needed to implement your proposed project.

Notes:

▪ Plan Project Development

In almost every industrial area, there are partially finished buildings and big pieces of equipment that have been there for years. They just sit there behind old fences while the wind whistles through their skeletons. Though each would have a different story to tell, they all represent large financial losses that often came from decisions that did not come out as expected. Decision management involves asking the right questions.

Develop Functional Proposal

Decision management involves knowing where you are going and how you are going to get there. It is important to have a proposal with identified and written detailed goals, needs, and resources.

√   Have the policies covering each activity been identified?

√   Does the proposal cover both normal operations and emergency preparedness?

Obtain Proposal Readiness Approval

In order to do a project, it is necessary to get everything ready, including the facilities, equipment, procedures, training, and people.

√   Are the activity goals and policies in keeping with the organization's goals and policies?

√ Does the proposal fit into the organization's normal operations?

√ Does the proposal conform to existing goals, policies, regulations, and codes?

√ Does the proposal for emergency preparedness fit into the organization's existing program?

√ Have appropriate management levels accepted the proposal for normal operations?

√ Have appropriate levels of management accepted the proposal for emergency preparedness procedures?

Get Facilities and Equipment Ready

Facilities and equipment include all of the space facilities, equipment, hardware, apparatus, and supplies—all the "things" needed to do the project or to make the proposed change. As part of this phase, specify, design, order, build, install, and test the operations and compatibility of all the "things" needed to do the project or make the change.

People must be able to safely make, install, use, maintain, and finally dispose of the material, supplies, tools, and equipment. Also, the equipment must work properly and be ergonomically designed to reduce physical stress on the operator.

Consider the following questions:

√ Has all of the equipment been installed and tested to meet the criteria for the new operations?

√ Does any of the new project's material or equipment require current equipment to exceed its electrical, mechanical, or chemical limits?

√ Do any of the materials or equipment require that people exceed their mental, physical, or emotional capabilities?

√ Are both the equipment and its operating and maintenance procedures ready for testing?

√ Is the space adequate to perform each of the activities needed to do the project or make the change?

Get Procedures and Training Ready

Review and rewrite the procedures and manuals or write new ones that describe all operations and equipment that is installed and used. These manuals must be written so that the instructions can be readily understood and followed by the people who use them. Training must cover the procedures and manuals for all operations and equipment used and it must be given to all those who are doing the jobs.

√ Have the procedures and training programs been written to cover all activity areas?

√ Have the procedures and training programs been written to cover the equipment and operations that will, in fact, be used?

√ Have the procedures and training programs been written so that the people who will use them can do so within their mental, physical, and emotional capabilities?

√ Have all heath and safety concerns been addressed?

√ Have all of the gender, customs, traditions, cultural and ethical taboos, and religious concerns that may affect the operations been considered?

In almost every organization, there are people who have difficulty in reading or understanding English. There are also many people who read at a very low level, and some who cannot read at all. Make sure the people who need the information can understand the training procedures and manuals. In today's multi-ethnic environment and in an expanding global business environment, the manuals and training must be in the local language and dialect of the people performing the tasks.

Get People Ready

In order to do a project, it may be necessary to get and train the right people. This may involve reassigning members of the existing staff or hiring a completely new staff for a new facility. Regardless of the number of people involved, the considerations are the same.

No matter how many jobs are involved, all are designed for and controlled by people—even the most complex or automated activity has a person in control. For people to work effectively, jobs must not require or invite people to exceed the safe limits of their mental, physical, or emotional capabilities. The job requirements are controlled by the design of the equipment and tasks, the way procedures and training programs are written and presented, and the way people work together. Remember that telling is not teaching.

To do their jobs consistently, safely, and well, people must work with equipment that is within their physical limits. Procedures must be within their mental capacities, and the work situation must be within their emotional limits.

√ Have the right people been selected for each task?

√ Have the people been trained to do their tasks?

√ Has the organizational structure been established?

√ Have personnel been assigned to specific tasks?

√ Have both technical and interpersonal training been conducted in order for the personnel to meet the goals?

√ Do the procedures and training address all of the gender, customs, tradition, cultural and ethical taboos, and religious concerns that may affect the employees?

Consider the material and questions in this section and list in the following space the major steps needed to implement your proposed project.

Notes:

▪ Plan System Integration

When the development phase of a new project has been approved, it must be integrated into the organization's ongoing operations. This will change the operational system. The change may be small, or it may have a considerable impact on the entire organization. The change will involve meeting the goals by having people work together to follow the procedures and use the equipment in keeping with the schedule and the budget. It also will involve adjusting to change. Before the change is made, consider the following evaluations:

Evaluate Effect on Goals and Policies

Since change may affect the organization's goals and policies, consider the following questions before the change and again after the change has been in effect for a time:

√ Have the activity goals remained viable?

√ Are all activities helping to meet the project goals?

√ Are all activities consistent with the project and the organization's policies?

√ Have any conditions changed which affect the importance of meeting the activity goals?

Evaluate Effect on Operational Schedules

Consider whether the change will affect the operational schedules.

- √ Do all activity areas use the same scheduling system?

- √ Is the scheduling system kept current with "real world" activities?

- √ Are the activities on schedule?

- √ Have changes in other areas affected the scheduling or scheduling system?

Evaluate Effect on Finances

Change will have an effect on the organization's finances. The effect may be positive or negative and may also affect both the short- and long-term financial picture.

Consider the following questions:

- √ Should the project be reconsidered because of recent changes in the market or in the organization's financial position?

- √ Will the effect of a change in finances or financial system be analyzed before being put into effect?

- √ How will changes in the budget affect the project?

√ Is each phase of the activity within its scheduled budget limits?

√ What effect will proposed changes in the activity have on the budget?

√ What effect will proposed changes in the activity have on the accounting system?

√ What effect will outside changes have on the activity's fiscal system or funding levels?

Evaluate Effect on Facilities and Equipment

Consider whether the equipment is being maintained properly.

√ Is the equipment performing as intended without exceeding its safe limits or the capabilities of people using it?

√ Will the proposed change in equipment adversely affect meeting other activity goals?

√ How will the change in equipment affect goals, schedules, finances, other equipment, procedures, training, and people?

√ How will changes in other phases of the activity affect equipment?

√ Will proposed changes affect the safety and efficiency of the operations?

Evaluate Effect on Procedures and Training Programs

Since change may have an effect on the procedures and the training programs, consider the following questions:

√ During actual operations, are the procedures being followed?

√ During operations, are the training programs being used to train new people and to refresh the knowledge and skills of the existing staff?

√ Have the procedures been reviewed by the users to ensure that they are understandable, accurate, and consistent with actual operations?

√ Have changes in other operations been reflected in adaptations to procedures and training?

√ Has the impact of changes in procedure or training affected other areas, such as goals and policies, schedules, finances, equipment, other procedures, training programs, and people?

Evaluate Effect on Personnel

The change may affect the personnel who are directly involved it as well as people in other parts of the organization.

√   Are people following the procedures to
perform their tasks?

√   Are personnel kept current on changes in
operations?

√   How will changes in personnel or job
assignments affect goals, policies, schedules,
finances, procedures, training, equipment,
and other personnel?

√   Do the procedures, training, and job
assignments address all of the gender,
customs, tradition, cultural and ethical
taboos, and religious concerns that may
affect the employees?

Consider the material and questions in this section
and list in the following space the major steps needed
to implement your proposed project.

Notes:

▪ Close Development Phase

Since all activities need to end someday, it is
important to prepare for closure. The end may mean
the complete stopping of an activity or operation, or it
may mean incorporating a change into normal
operational procedures. Evaluate the following
considerations when getting ready to phase out an
operation:

Stop Project Development Phase

There are two different reasons to stop the development phase of a project. Either the project is completed and has been integrated into the system, or the project is not going to be used. If a project is not to be used, the development phase should not just fade away; it should be stopped. The information developed thus far in the project development should be documented so that if the proposal is reconsidered at a later date, the data is available.

To illustrate this point, there is an old story (of dubious origin) about a gentleman whose job it was to stand at the foot of a flight of stairs in the British Parliament building. As was often the custom, he had inherited the job many years before when his father retired. During a fiscal crunch, someone asked why he stood there. He said, "Because it is my job." They then searched out the man's aging father and asked him why he had stood there for so many years. He said that long ago he was assigned to stand there to remind people to watch out for fresh paint. Since no one had ever told him to do something else, he just kept standing there until he retired. Although probably not true, there is a grain of truth in the story. Many of us have seen projects go on long after there was no longer a real need.

Evaluate Effect on Goals and Policies

By considering some of the following questions during the planning for closing out a project or operation, it may be possible to learn from some of its mistakes. If you are planning to incorporate the project into normal operations, consider the following questions to ensure that oversights are avoided during the transition:

√ Upon completion, did the activity meet the goals?

√ During the life of the activity, were the policies followed?

√ After an interim change, have the goals and policies been updated?

√ Are updated goals and policies still in keeping with the organization's goals and policies?

√ At the end of the project, are the original and updated goals and policies included in the project's final report?

Evaluate Effect on Schedule

√ Have the scheduling goals been met at the end of the activity?

√ Have records of the scheduling program been included in the final report?

√ Have changes been incorporated into normal operations without adversely affecting the ability of the organization to meet its goals?

Evaluate Effect on Finances

√ At the end of the activity or after a funding change, has the closure of the fiscal system been planned so that there is proper use of any excess money?

√ Are the accounting records balanced and closed?

√ Are there adequate records for a fiscal audit of all phases of the activities?

Evaluate Effect on Equipment

√ At the end of the activity, have all supplies and equipment been safely and economically disposed of?

√ When the change has been incorporated into normal operations, has an operational readiness test been completed and approved?

Evaluate Effect on Procedures and Training

√ At the completion of a change, has it been incorporated into normal operations?

√ At the completion of a change, has it been incorporated into emergency preparedness procedures?

Evaluate Effect on Personnel

√ Have personnel been updated on the change?

√ Have personnel who are no longer needed for
the activity been dismissed or placed in other
jobs?

Consider the material and questions in this section
and list in the following space the major steps needed
to implement your proposed project.

Notes:

Develop Opportunities for New Projects

Some people who have entrepreneurial skill and drive like to be in charge of taking their new ideas from conception to reality. It is important to make it advantageous for them to do this within the organization. Instead of leaving the company to start new ventures, project developers can create profitable new projects within the company.

▪ Start Internal Profit Centers

The big advantage of an internal profit center is that it has the resources of a big organization and the independence of a small company. For this reason, many people would prefer not to start their own business. Internal profit centers can create a climate where everyone wins.

However, an internal profit center may not be right for either the proposed project or the organization. Some organizations do help their people start their own business. They may let the person go on leave and may offer financing and technical assistance. If the new endeavor succeeds, the company makes a profit from its investment. If it fails, the person comes back with strengthened company loyalty. This can be a situation where everyone wins. The idea may also be developed to the point where it can be sold to another organization.

Consider the material in this section and in the following space list some of the steps that can be taken to ensure that there are opportunities for new projects.

Notes:

6 - Encourage Employees' Ideas

In almost all organizations, there are creative people who enjoy playing with new ideas. Though these people may have many good and useful new ideas, they may be unwilling to share their ideas with the organization. Your effective encouragement of everyone's creative talents can turn many of these new ideas into profits.

Acknowledging the need for new ideas and creating a nurturing environment are vital in getting people to bring their ideas forward. Managers and coworkers must acknowledge the importance of creativity so that people feel comfortable playing with their new ideas. When creative people feel that it is okay to play with new ideas, they are more willing to share their thoughts and often generate ideas in others. You can go even further by openly encouraging people to work on new ideas.

However, to benefit, you must be willing to listen to all new ideas, although some may seem ridiculous. Even when people present what at first may appear to be ridiculous ideas, they deserve credit for making the suggestion.

This chapter covers some of the things that you can do to get all the people on teams to make creative suggestions.

Encourage Everyone to Suggest Ideas

Managers may face a major conflict when soliciting new ideas. They either must be willing to accept an incomplete new idea or to accept only completely finished reports. How managers handle this conflict will influence how people will make suggestions for ways to improve the organization, its products, or its services.

▪ Management Support

Some managers will accept only perfection and will return reports to subordinates because they are not perfect. I knew a manager who read every letter or report with a red pencil in his hand. He would circle spelling, grammar, or factual errors, and after the third error would throw the document in the wastebasket. He said that if the writer did not care enough about the report to correct the errors, he must not have felt the report had much value. Since he considered the writer felt it was of little value, he saw no reason to read it. This attitude can create problems when evaluating the returns on time investment. Consider that there may be a middle ground between mediocrity and perfection.

The general manager may reasonably not have enough time to spend on a first draft report of a new idea. However, the supervisor of the person submitting the report needs to take time to evaluate the first draft of a new idea. If the idea has potential merit, spend more time developing it. However, if the new idea has little merit, do not spend time developing a complete and perfect report only to have it rejected.

This is essentially quality control. Reject things at the lowest possible level. A rough draft is of less value than a finished report. Improve quality control by reevaluating written or unwritten policies that imply that rough draft proposals should be discarded without consideration. Handwritten ideas and sketches on a notepad is the least expensive way to evaluate a proposed new idea. At this point if it looks reasonable, write a more detailed proposal for the next evaluation step.

▪ Improve the Present System

Many organizations have so many policies "against everything" that it is almost impossible to make any changes. These restrictive policies imply that the employees cannot be trusted to use good judgment. People do not like to be told by someone or by policies that they cannot be trusted. Demeaning people does not encourage them to do outstanding work.

Most people want to do a good job, and they will if they are given a chance. They like to work for an organization they can be proud of, and they also want to make it a better place to work. People are not afraid of hard work! Notice how many work hard on their yards, home improvement, hobbies, supporting political or volunteer causes, attending classes, sewing, or writing.

With good management and encouragement, people in your work group can develop new ideas about ways to improve the organization's profit and change its impact on the environment and the community. However, they cannot develop these ideas if they are always pushed to complete yesterday's assignments. Excellence does take time!

▪ Allow Enough Time for New Ideas

People need to feel free to set aside some time to think and talk about new ideas. Sometimes when managers see a few people talking, they assume that they are not talking about work. It also will not be effective to say, "Every Tuesday at 2:30 p.m. you may take ten minutes to think about new ideas." People generally get new ideas when they are having a problem doing a job. That is when the sudden "why not do it this way?" idea pops into their heads. Discuss ideas promptly, or they may be lost. I think we have all experienced the exasperating feeling of being interrupted and then forgetting what we wanted to say. Just talking about a new idea for a few minutes may be all that is needed to help fix the idea in our thought process.

Allow flextime so new ideas can be evaluated before they are lost. Perhaps this will require only enough time to write down the idea so that it is not forgotten. It takes time to obtain, analyze, and synthesize data, to "sell" a concept and to get the idea started. Zero time may produce zero ideas. After evaluating the initial idea, if it still seems to be a good idea, it will take more time and money to develop it to the point where it is ready for the next approval step. For more information on the development and approval steps, see **Chapter 3 – Decide Which Ideas to Use.**

▪ Develop a Special R&D Budget in Each Department

One way to be able to develop new ideas is to use a small specific budget for this purpose. Some companies have a special budget for technical managers to use, and these projects are "off-the-record." However, limiting the discretionary budget to only technical managers implies that non-technical managers do not have any valuable ideas. The second problem is that if a failed project is "off-the-record," what did not work will not be recorded. Not recording projects means that several different managers may try out the same "new" idea and fail repeatedly. However, if they know where someone else failed, they may not try it, or they may be able to see how they can do it differently. Evaluate both the obvious and the questionable failures in order to avoid future failures and find some benefit in the failure.

In order to use the information from both successes and failures, it is necessary to have a good communication network.

▪ Improve the Communication Network

Many old-time rigid bureaucratic managers are comfortable with only top-down communications or at best think all communications must be by memo up and down the "proper" chain of command. I have heard people discuss working in a rigid bureaucracy where they were not allowed to talk to a person in a different work group even though they were both working on the same project. An inefficient communication system destroys any spontaneity for developing new ideas that could result from the interaction between two different specialists.

Bureaucracy stifles spontaneity, creativity, and growth. Many organizations are replacing the old bureaucratic layers with more natural networking between people. In many organizations, networking is the management style of choice. Some of these organizations are in a position to influence the structure and management styles of other companies. This style utilizes networks, small teams, and other decentralized structures. Bureaucracy may always be with us, but its rigid controlling powers will decrease in forward-looking organizations.

In a free-flowing networking system, ideas can be exchanged, and through the exchange process more new ideas can emerge. In a networking environment, people learn from peers; everyone is a resource for everyone else, and there is a continuous interaction among employees. A decision to act can be made only when enough good data backs up the decision. Failure to initiate actions aimed at growth is a far more serious failure than running slightly over on an expense budget in order to bring in a needed program. Growth comes from the development of new ideas.

There are several types of actions needed to get new ideas flowing in a work group. The more new ideas that flow, the more likely some of those ideas will be of significance. How people feel about the organization can make a difference in how much they are willing to risk to develop new ideas for it. It takes some entrepreneurial spirit to develop ideas. When new projects are done within an organization, the organization can take some risk out of development and gain some of the benefits. How people are rewarded for their efforts can make a difference in whether they are willing to give their new ideas to the organization for which they work, withhold them, or develop them for their own benefit.

Consider the material and questions in this section and list in the following space the major steps needed to implement your proposed project.

Notes:

Reward New Ideas (even if they don't work)

Many organizations set up committees to devise ways to improve their operations. Some of these committees are successful while others never seem to find anything that needs improving. A young man who was working his way through college as a waiter in a large chain restaurant told how he learned about business politics. Apparently, it was company policy for each restaurant to have a committee of employees to find ways to improve service. His boss told him to serve on committee and make a list of things that could be improved. Since he was a business major, he was able to pinpoint many needed changes. As instructed, he kept his list confidential and turned it in to his boss. His reward for doing a thorough and conscientious job: he was reprimanded for being a "troublemaker." Of course, he made no more suggestions, though they told him to stay on the committee. He learned that what his boss wanted and his boss's boss wanted were two different things.

Rewards must make the person receiving them feel good. If an individual feels good about the reward, she or he will seek more rewards. If the reward makes only the giver feel good, then it has lost its purpose.

How rewards are used can sometimes do more harm than good. Most people have an intrinsic desire to do a good job. However, when we become conditioned to the extrinsic motivation to getting rewards, our intrinsic motivation may be reduced. This is especially true of creative activities, which are intrinsically motivated.

Potentially even more destructive consequences of using rewards can occur when people expect a reward and do not get it. At that point, they may be resentful or angry, and they have now significantly lost motivation to contribute. Something that makes most employees angry is when the company asks them to take a cut in pay because of hard times, and then top management gives itself huge bonuses. The newspapers tell of CEOs who have run their companies into bankruptcy and at the same time received millions of dollars in bonuses. When this happens, it is hard not to be bitter toward management.

I have known people who have been bitter toward the organization for years because someone else got the reward they thought should have been theirs. As a result, they channeled their creative input into destructive activities toward the organization. It is appalling the amount of damage that some people have done to organizations where they have worked. Two books I recommend for every manager, even though I find them both almost frightening to read, are *Punished by Rewards*, by Alfie Kohn,[4] and *Sabotage in the American Workplace: Anecdotes of Dissatisfaction, Mischief and Revenge*, edited by

---

[4] Kohn, Alfie. *Punished by Rewards*. New York: Houghton Mifflin, 1993.

Martin Sprouse.[5] Kohn's book develops the case against some types of reward systems, and Sprouse's book is a collection of stories about real people doing real revenge damage to their companies.

▪ Types of Rewards

The types of rewards that are given will depend on what the reward is intended to accomplish and the nature of the contributions the individual or team made to the organization. Rewards can range from a direct compliment, to a letter of acknowledgment in a personnel file, to a favorable comment in work group meetings, to public recognition, to extra financial compensation.

Percentage of Profit Rewards

When a new idea results in the organization's making more money, a person may feel he or she should also get more money. When the amount of money involved can be identified, many organizations give the person who had the idea a percentage of the profits for a given number of years.

One-Time Bonus Rewards

Sometimes the new idea may increase production, make a job easier, or create safer work conditions. In

---

[5] Sprouse, Martin, editor. *Sabotage in the American Workplace: Anecdotes of Dissatisfaction, Mischief and Revenge.* San Francisco, CA: Pressure Drop Press, 1992.

these instances, it may be hard to determine exactly how much money is made or saved. When this happens, some organizations give a lump sum payment for the idea. In some cases, it is hard to determine just who should get the reward; one person may have had the original idea, but the idea may have grown and changed as many others were involved in its development. When this happens, the people involved may be the best ones to determine how any financial reward should be divided among those in the group. However, this could get out of hand if not handled properly.

Extra money is always welcome. In some cases, if we do not get a financial reward, we may feel cheated by the organization. Yet the financial reward, particularly if it is small, may not be cherished as much as other types of rewards.

Patent Rights

In some organizations, individuals may receive the patent rights to certain types of inventions, while the organization maintains the right to produce and control the invention for a given number of years.

Praise from Support System

Compliments from people whom we respect carry considerable weight in encouraging people to do a good job. Announcing in a work group meeting that a person or a group of people did something extra special, and that it was appreciated, can make them feel very good.

There is one caution about giving praise in front of a group. I have known people who do a good job but who are reclusive and would be uncomfortable being rewarded in front of a group. They would much prefer to receive any rewards in private with only a few close friends present. I know a man who, after thirty-seven years of work, refused to have a retirement luncheon in his honor. He and a few close friends went to lunch, and that was it.

Praise from Management

Many people would feel good about getting praise from "Mr. or Ms. Big." Many would like to get their praise in front of their friends. It would be much better for "Mr. or Ms. Big" to come to the work group meeting than for the work group to go to the front office to receive the reward. When a manager comes to the work group, work integration occurs.

Organizational Recognition

I have a friend who was told by her supervisor that she was going with him to the company's annual rewards luncheon. She felt she had too much work to do, but he insisted, so she went. At the luncheon she received, much to her surprise, a special reward for some work she had done. She was embarrassed to get up in front of a large gathering of management and have the president give her the reward. Fortunately, she had had enough experience in public speaking and enough self-confidence that she was able to gracefully handle the situation. However, she would have been much more comfortable if she had known that the reward was coming. Many people like surprises; others do not and would have dreaded being required to get up in front of the president of the company. Such a person may remember the embarrassment more vividly than the reward, as was the case in this instance.

In such a case, the presentation of the reward may do more harm than good. Many managers are in management because they like the spotlight. This does not mean that everyone likes public recognition. Know your people and reward them accordingly. If in doubt, ask a close friend of the person who is being rewarded. In the case of the man with thirty-seven years of service, we asked his close friends and called his daughter. They all said that he would much prefer a simple luncheon with just a few friends. He was not even comfortable when the department head stopped by the shop and said a few good words. The reward is for the person getting the reward, not just to make management feel good.

Public Recognition

Major accomplishments can also receive public acknowledgment. A short piece in the company publication or in the local newspaper can be a significant acknowledgment. Except for the cost of a photo and writing the article, there is no cost to the organization, but the reward to the organization can be great. People and their friends feel good about their part in the public image of the organization as a great place to work. The better people feel about an organization, the more they want to help the organization prosper. This is true of people both inside and outside the organization. Outside the organization, customers may be one of the best information sources on how to improve a product; after all, they are the users.

Professional Journals

Descriptive articles in professional journals on completed new projects are an ego boost for most people. Having an article published in a professional journal may have an added benefit; working with the organization's technical writers may improve the individual's writing skills and confidence.

Professional Meetings

It is also an ego boost for most people to make a presentation of their pet project at a professional meeting. This too may have the added benefit of helping them develop skill and confidence as a speaker.

Reward Ideas That Can't Be Used

Of course, you cannot use all ideas, and some will not even work. However, reward these ideas. The purpose of the rewards is to help people feel good about their efforts to help the organization whether or not they succeed. Thanking people for their participation is a way to show your appreciation.

Private Feedback

Most people do not expect anything more than a simple "thank you" for making a suggestion, but they do expect at least that much. I know there have been times when I have made suggestions and the most I got was a grunt. There were other times when I got laughter—and that hurt.

On one occasion, I was asked to comment on the long-term development path of a project. Since I was aware that my ideas were different from those of the person asking for my opinion, I detailed the logic I used in my prediction. In a later discussion about my comments, I was told in a laughing manner, "You just don't understand what is going on around here." A number of years later, the manager who had laughed at my projection admitted that I had been right, but by then the damage had been done, and for me the recognition came too late. By being open to how another person looks at a situation, you might be able to use his or her suggestions or help make their idea work.

Suggestions to Expand an Idea

If the idea does not look like it will work as presented, suggest ways it can be expanded so it might work in a different situation. If an idea is a good one and your organization cannot use it, it may be worth developing to the point where it could be sold to an organization that could use it. Some organizations have encouraged the development of small, self-contained companies within the organization's existing structure. Companies use these satellite operations to develop a new product or service. This structure has the advantage of both the resources of the larger organization and the flexibility of a small company.

Suggestions to Adapt an Idea

It may be possible to modify or adapt an idea to work in a different situation. "We have always done it that way!" is one of the best reasons to question procedures. Sometimes even a slight change in how a procedure is followed can save time and increase production. For instance, someone may question the distribution list for a specific report. This question raises the issue of whether anyone ever reads the report. I know I have stayed on distribution lists long after I needed the original information. I could have called someone and been taken off the list, but most of the time I just chucked the report into the recycling bin, a total waste of everyone's time and an unnecessary degradation of the environment.

When one distribution list has an error, it may be worth checking all distribution lists of the reports your group distributes. Even though this requires an expenditure of time, eventually it saves time because you are not sending out as many copies. Those not receiving the report will appreciate the time you save them because they don't have to handle the report. It is easy to just add someone to an email list, but it takes time for the receiver of the email to evaluate the material. One way to improve email distribution is with a short descriptive subject heading. If people then decide to open the email, there can be a short paragraphs describing the report or reports with a download command. This way the person receiving the email uses the least possible time to evaluate the report. There should also be a "delete me from distribution" command in every distribution email.

A number of years ago, as part of a new job assignment, I inherited the responsibility for a monthly report that took a lot of time to prepare and had a wide distribution. I was concerned that the report was a waste of time, but my boss felt that everyone on the list wanted the information. The next time I sent out the report I included a cover letter explaining that we were updating our distribution list and to send back the letter if they wanted to continue receiving the report. I waited and waited, but I never received any requests for the report. I then stopped sending out the report, with the boss's permission, and no one ever complained.

Reconsideration of a Reworked Idea

A reworked idea may have some real potential and may be worth reconsideration. However, some people may not be skilled at recognizing hidden potential. If you do not tend to see hidden potential within a vague idea, there may be people in your group who are good at seeing the essence of the new idea within what may appear to be a lot of fog. Search out these people and use them as sounding boards. The few hours they spend evaluating the reworked idea can have two advantages. First, they may be able to identify and clarify an idea that could bring an excellent return on investment. Second, it makes people feel that someone welcomes their ideas and encourages them to present any that may help the organization. It is a good investment if it can help break the feeling of "Why say anything? They won't do anything anyway!"

Even ideas that cannot be used or will not work need to be acknowledged and people rewarded for submitting the idea. If the "pat on the back" helps them feel better about their job and their organization, it is a worthwhile investment of time and effort for the manager. Such encouragement can produce more suggestions.

Consider the material in this section and in the following space suggest ways to improve the reward system in your work group.

Notes:

▪ Acknowledge Need for New Ideas

I think we have all been told, "Never give advice unless asked." Unfortunately, that saying is ingrained in most of us. We tend not to make suggestions or offer advice unless we truly believe it is wanted. When a person asks you, "How do you like my new _____?," we have all learned that the best answer is complimentary. If we want feedback on suggestions, we need to make sure people believe we want their advice. Words are often not enough; it takes action to show them that we are willing not only to listen but to encourage their comments, both negative and positive.

Little New Ideas Are Important

There are many areas where little changes can make a big difference in the cost, quality, or volume of the organization's output. The output may be clean floors for the custodian, supplies on time for the purchasing agent, or a clarification of corporate goals for the president. Suggestions on how to get the floors cleaner, get supplies on time, or clarify a goal may be little suggestions, but when they produce results they can improve the organization's performance.

Decrease Activity and Increase Output

Activities are what we do; the output is what we produce, and that is what is important. It has been said that activity will increase to fill up the time available. If it is the activity that is being evaluated and not the output, it is easy for a person to just appear to be busy. I have heard people say that all you need to do is have a clipboard in your hand, walk very fast, and have a determined look on your face, and no one will question what you are doing.

Requesting that people look at ways to decrease inefficient activities and increase output can clarify what their job is. For example, if now means immediately, then NOW is to be observed. However, when things are always needed NOW, quality can suffer. All activities are not the same priority to everyone. I have seen many variations of the poster, "Poor Planning on Your Part Does Not Make Your Request a High Priority for Me."

Increase Management Effectiveness

Managers can increase their effectiveness in a number of ways. One good way is to encourage others to make suggestions that will help the organization improve. For example, we may ask someone to do a task but then never let go of it and always be looking over his or her shoulder. Or we may give someone a job that we don't like and never check on how he or she is doing, thus abdicating our responsibility for follow-through. Specific ongoing suggestions can improve our effectiveness.

Reduce Equipment Downtime

When things do go wrong, as in the case of unscheduled equipment downtime, it can be very expensive, especially when it happens in the middle of a run. Proper preventive maintenance and emergency preplanning can reduce unscheduled down-time.

For example, the silicon chip wafer manufacturing process uses some very toxic chemicals. Many of these chemicals are gases under pressure. If there is a leak, the engineers need to shut down the system and evacuate the work area. Emergency crews in protective clothing need to go in and fix the leak and get the facility ready for reoccupancy—a very expensive leak.

To prevent this problem, some companies put the gas lines inside an outer pipe with an airflow to a toxic gas monitor. The airflow is exhausted in the same way as the exhaust from the equipment. In this way, if there is a leak of toxic gas, it is safely exhausted through the outer pipe. The automatic gas monitor notifies maintenance personnel so they can take appropriate action. However, the workstation does not have to be shut down because the leak is safely contained. The engineers can then schedule maintenance so that there is minimal loss of productive time. Preplanning averts possible problems so that time and materials are not wasted.

Reduce Waste

Every dollar of waste that can be prevented is pure profit for the organization. At a ten percent profit margin, the organization must sell ten dollars worth of products in order to make one dollar in profit; put another way, one dollar saved is worth ten dollars in sales.

Waste comes either from a normal byproduct of a process or from damage. There are two ways to reduce waste: (1) do not generate it in the first place, and (2) use the waste as raw material for input to a different process.

Change the process and sell the byproduct. For example, the scrap from a machine shop can be sorted, collected, and sold. If it is sorted as it is generated, it is easier to collect, and sorted scrap materials sell at higher prices. In this case, the scrap is at the lowest possible cost to the company. If, however, the finished piece is damaged and it goes into the scrap, the cost to the company is much higher. It may be possible to modify your process so the byproduct is of high value to some other organization. You may also be able to use the byproduct of some other company. This is often done in civil engineering projects where one company will have excess landfill and another contractor will need landfill. By coordinating their jobs, they both save money.

Every effort should be made to avoid damage to materials; the further along in the process damage occurs, the greater the loss. In many companies, the operators are women who are about five feet tall. However, men who were six feet tall designed some of the equipment. There are cases where the short women have difficulty reaching high controls, and because they do not have stepstools, it causes setting errors. It turns out to be a very expensive decision not to buy stools or make work platforms. In addition to the materials damaged, people can also be injured.

Reduce Injuries

People endure pain and suffering from an injury. There are two additional types of losses to organizations when someone is injured. An incidence of serious injury wastes time because other employees stand around watching and continue talking about what happened long after it is over. There is also the additional time needed for the accident investigation and the ensuing reports.

The second loss is of staff to do the job. Even though not all employees are there all the time, you can plan training, meetings, and vacations. But an injury is unplanned and takes employees off the job. It may cause a slowdown in one area which, in just-in-time production schedules, can have a ripple effect on many other areas. Accidents can be very expensive! An accident takes away from profit as clearly as if the money were stolen from the safe.

Reduce Crime

Corporate crime is a growing concern and can range from an employee taking a few small items to multimillion-dollar losses. We all know that there are criminals "out there" but not in our company. The sad truth is that people who steal are everywhere. Some are kleptomaniacs and just cannot seem to help themselves; others are skilled criminals. Everyone in the organization must be made aware that theft can contribute to a major loss of revenue.

The key element for crime is opportunity; if criminals can get it, they will take it. It has been said that everyone has a price. I like the story of the woman who said she just could not understand why prostitutes would participate in sex for money. A man asked her if she would go to bed with him for a million dollars, and she said yes. He then asked if she would do it for ten dollars, and she said, "What do you think I am?" He said, "What you are has already been established. We're now just haggling over the price." Given the opportunity, some people do have a price.

There are people who feel that it is a crime only if what is stolen is something of real monetary value. I have heard kids say that they never shoplift; they say they take candy and stuff like that, but they never steal anything. Little things do cost a lot of money when added up. The supply departments in many large organizations know that in September people use a lot more office supplies or school supplies than during the rest of the year. People do steal supplies, small parts, tools and other little things; that cost comes directly out of profit.

Managers must be alert to crime; that does not mean that they should assume everyone is a thief. It is important to reduce the opportunity for theft so you can keep honest employees honest and deter the dishonest. By being open to suggestions and discussing the problem of crime, people become more alert and are encouraged to speak up when they see something that does not look right.

Some criminals are very bold, and because they are, they are often not noticed. There was a case where new equipment was being installed in a new office building. Some men came in, all dressed alike with the supplier's name on their uniforms. They told the security guard that there had been a mix-up in the delivery and that they needed to take back some of the new office equipment; they would be back in about an hour. You guessed it! They never came back because they did not work for the supplier. No one checked for paperwork, and the guard even held the door for them.

That type of bold theft is harder to spot than you would expect. When I was teaching at Cogswell College in San Francisco, the college was in an old building that had heating tanks of oil in reserve for the furnaces. One day I walked out and saw a heating oil truck with the hose in the tank. I never gave it a second thought; the building maintenance man also saw the same truck and thought nothing of it. It turned out that the man was sucking oil out of a tank and putting it into his truck. The storage tank was not locked, and no one had asked the truck driver what he was doing because the theft was so bold and unexpected. There was no insurance for that loss.

Even with insurance, not all losses are covered. Take, for example, the major loss to a small business that lost all of its office equipment and computers in one night. In addition to alarms on the doors and windows, there was a walking security guard on the premises. However, the burglars were able to bypass the alarms by going up the access ladder to the crawl space between the roof and the ceiling and down into the office through the ceiling; they then took the materials out the same way. Their insurance company replaced the equipment, and the ceiling was repaired and the crawl space secured. The business lost more than a week of production time for the entire staff; this loss of time was not covered by insurance, nor was the loss of the records on the computer hard drives, though they did have some backup data.

Insurance is not enough; prevention is also needed. The security department or consultants can give general guidelines and set up a prevention program. However, ideas about prevention and detection can come from the people who work in the area; they may be your best source of information. They may see a jimmied window or notice a shortage in the inventory or something that just looks "funny," like someone they have never seen before just looking around. Setting an attitude about theft can also make a difference. Someone once told me that where they worked, pay was the combination of your salary and all you could steal. Managers can change that attitude to one where theft is not tolerated.

Consider the material and questions in this section and list in the following space any suggestions to improve your workplace.

Notes:

New Ideas Can Come from Everyone

People do their jobs in the work area; they know when things are not right, and they often know when and how to make things better. The person who does the job knows the job best.

People Doing the Jobs

If people are having trouble doing a job efficiently, it may be the job that is wrong and not the person. People can tell you problems that they are having on the job without actually saying anything. Watch the person do the job. If five-foot-tall women have trouble reaching a control or seeing a dial, they may make errors that are not their fault. If employees say they do not understand the manual, it is possible that the manual needs to be rewritten. If they keep making errors that require some academic skills, the job may not be right for the people hired for the job. If people are tense and high-strung at the end of the day, maybe the job is putting too much stress on them.

Listen to what people say to you and to each other about ways to improve the job. Also, listen to what they do not say in words but may say in actions, i.e., slamming down a tool that is hard to use or rubbing a sore arm.

Coworkers

A coworker may tell you that someone else is having trouble with a job. Of course, if you go to that person and say, "She said you couldn't do your job very well! You don't have any trouble, do you?" you may not improve things. That is what Andrew Grove, in his book *High Output Management*, calls negative leverage because it takes very little effort to make things a lot worse.[6]

Encourage people to share their problems. Because some people are reluctant to ask, other people may be willing and able to make suggestions to help them do their job and improve output while decreasing the physical, mental, and/or emotional strain on them. Obviously, this must be done strategically to be effective.

Managers

One very good source of suggestions for improvement can come from other managers. When managers look over each other's areas, one person can help spot things the other does not see.

Purchasing Personnel

The people in the purchasing department may be able to help you buy more efficiently. For example, you may

---

[6] Grove, Andrew. *High Output Management*. New York: Random House, 1995.

need ten items a month so you order ten items a month. If asked, the purchasing agent may be able to tell you that the item comes a dozen to a box. Since you never received a full box, you did not know that a dozen costs the same as ten. They may also be able to help you save money by suggesting different materials that may be cheaper but work just as well.

Research and Development Personnel

The research and development (R&D) professionals may be able to help you solve a specific problem. In addition, you may be able to help them with a new product design by telling them how your specialty will be involved with the final product.

Health and Safety Personnel

The health and safety professionals can offer suggestions on the reduction of hazards in your work area. However, they are not mind readers; unless you tell them, they may not know that you have started to use, for example, a different chemical. Call them and ask for advice about a hazard before there is an accident. Not only invite but also insist that they do routine inspections of your work area. They are specialists in spotting hazards that you may have overlooked or may not recognize as hazards. The objective is to focus on preventing expensive accidents.

Waste Disposal Personnel

Waste disposal is expensive, especially when the waste is hazardous. By working with the waste disposal specialist, it may be possible to sell some of the waste. That creates a double profit; you save by not paying for disposal, and someone pays you to take it away.

Suppliers

Suppliers also need to make a profit, and a happy customer brings them more sales. They may be able to show you how you can save money by using different products. The new product may even cost more but save money because it will last longer. Low bid is not always the best buy.

End-Product Users

End-product users know best whether your product or service fits their needs. They may have some excellent suggestions for improvements in your product; many suggestions may come from product or services users if the information is requested. It is important to give credit where credit is due. When a sales representative gets an idea from a customer, it should be rewarded. If the improvement simply makes the job easier for the customer and there is no measurable financial gain for the producer, a letter of appreciation to the customer would help build the company's reputation. If there were a financial gain for the producer, then a letter and a financial reward might encourage more suggestions.

If we feel we have been treated unfairly, we may have some strong negative feelings about a company. I worked part-time on a farm when I was in college. Part of my job was to mow weeds using a mowing machine with a sickle bar, but because of the high weeds, the sickle bar would hit rocks and break the blades. I then had to stop and replace the broken blades. To prevent this from happening, I built a special guard that kept the sickle bar higher off the ground and thus prevented blade breakage. One day, when I was in the farm equipment store getting more blades, the factory sales representative was there, so I showed him what I had built and asked if the company was interested. He said, "No, not unless you have a patent." As a college student, I did not have a patent or the money to get one. However, the next year the company came out with a new sickle bar guard that was standard. Of course, it was much nicer than mine, but it worked the same way. The development of their new product could have been coincidental, but I do not think so, and I think the sales representative got credit for my invention.

Be aware that any payment or agreement you make must be cleared through the legal department.

▪ Suggestion Committees

When people work together to develop suggestions for improvements, their ideas tend to build on each other's so that in the end, better suggestions are generated.

In a cooperative work group, people can feel free to help each other and make suggestions on ways to change the job to do it more efficiently and/or generate more output. This benefit comes from management's trust of the people in the work groups and its willingness to empower them to have choices and control.

Consider the material in this section and in the following space suggest areas that could be a source of new ideas.

Notes:

Organizational Attitudes Start at the Top

Some managers do not seem to like cooperation and prefer to encourage contention among their subordinates. I know a schoolteacher who has worked for years in a school where people with "new" ideas were highly praised by the principal. However, they got no credit for sharing ideas. The result was that teachers stole ideas from each other and called them their own. With credit only for new ideas and not for sharing, there began to develop a caste system among the teachers. As in any caste system, some of the teachers felt they could gain a sense of self-worth only by discrediting the others. All the while, the administration seemed either oblivious of what was going on or positively supported it.

The lack of recognition of our special abilities may reduce our desire to make suggestions for improvement. We may not even want to give a fair day's work. The operating environment of a firm controls results. Do not expect changes in results if you have not changed the conditions. People need to know what the organization wants from them.

Published Organizational Goals and Policies

Most organizations have published organizational goals. However, these may not have been updated for years. In other cases, written documents are vague and lofty goals that do not fit the reality of what is really happening in today's business climate.

To be effective, goals and policies must be flexible enough to fit changing situations. I remember a friend who sent his application to a college and had it returned with a letter explaining that the college now had a new policy that, to assure delivery, only applications sent by registered mail would be accepted. Of course, by the time he sent the letter back, he had to pay a late fee. To be effective, policies must be realistic, and they must be flexible.

Actions by Management to Support Goals and Policy

To produce effective results, goals must be supported at all levels of management. I know a young man who worked for a small company that sells spas. Having worked his way through college, he was used to long hours and working seven days a week. His first assignment was to open a new store and get it ready for business; the president went over what needed to be done and left on a business trip. A few days later, the vice president of the company came to the store to review the assignment and said to the young man, "But are you having fun?" Together they rewrote one of their company's goals so that you could have fun while making money.

Budgeted Time and Money

The philosophy of "put your money where your mouth is" can be applied to the organizational goal of encouraging everyone to make suggestions for improvement. Yet when people are told by their manager that the company does not have the time or the money to work on a new idea, they know how hollow that policy really is. Some organizations have a small discretionary budget that managers can use for new idea development; others assume that the managers will spend only the amount of money needed to run their operation. Goals are effective only if they are actually used as guidelines.

Budgeted Reward System

Having time and money set aside for a reward system can make it easier for managers to set up a valid system for rewards. The worst possible system is one that is inconsistent. I know of one organization that was undergoing a reduction in force and many people were taking early retirement. The first group to take the retirement received a nice engraved plaque upon retirement. Then management decided the plaques were too expensive, so the next group received a form letter thanking them for their long years of service. Needless to say, the second group was very unhappy, and the people who stayed may well wonder what will happen when they retire.

Consider the material in this section and in the following space suggest ways that management could encourage new ideas.

Notes:

Encourage Everybody to Play with New Ideas

Some people like to play with new ideas and ways to do things. They want to enjoy their work, and they want more out of work than just a paycheck. Yet some managers try to kill any attempts at improving the work environment. I once had a boss who was quick to find fault and slow to praise. To make that point he had a sign in his office that read: "One aw-shit wipes out 100 attaboys." I like to play with new ideas, but this did not encourage me to take risks and try ideas that might not turn out as I expected.

However, many other things do encourage playing with new ideas. When people have fun exploring ideas, they are more likely to develop and present usable suggestions.

▪ Work Group Praise

The work group is the nucleus of the organization's culture. The work group is like a family in the same way the organization is like a community. Like families, some work groups are harmonious while others are dysfunctional and filled with strife and hostility. The synergetic efforts of cooperative and harmonious work groups can produce more effective new ideas than groups where there is conflict among members. When managers believe in the importance of cooperative idea development, they can praise the efforts of the group and thus generate more ideas to improve their jobs, their products, or their services. This praise can be given to small groups as they work on an idea or to the larger assembled group upon its completion.

Staff Meetings

In staff meetings, the progress of a developing idea can be discussed and additional input encouraged. The staff meeting is also an effective place for an "attaboy" to praise the progress of a group working on an idea.

Bulletin Board and Website Notices

A brief progress report may be posted on the bulletin board in the work area or on the employee-only part of the company website. This will let people know what is happening, which in turn may produce an idea to help the group develop the new idea.

Posted Letters to Management

When a supervisor sends a letter to management praising an individual, a copy can be posted to let the work group know that management does appreciate the development of new ideas.

Consider the material in this section and in the following space suggest ways to encourage employees to develop new ideas.

Notes:

Encourage Creative People to Share New Ideas

There may be more exceptionally creative people in the organization than management knows about. Many of these people have jobs that do not require the use of their creative talent. They themselves may not even be aware that they have an exceptional talent; they may think that everyone likes to think about new ideas. They may also be painfully aware that they think of many new ideas that are beyond the imagination of others. When they have been laughed at and ridiculed to excess, creative people may keep quiet and never tell anyone about their ideas.

▪ Never Laugh at Ridiculous Ideas

The creative people in your group who offer what may seem like ridiculous ideas need to be encouraged to keep offering all their ideas. Some of these ideas may not be as ridiculous as they first sound and may really be of great economic value. What may seem to be ridiculous today may be commonplace tomorrow. If you look back, a great deal that we take as commonplace today started as a ridiculous idea. I am sure that the person who first suggested many of these ideas heard others say, "Why would anyone want to do that?"

The other advantage of the ridiculous idea is that it may spark a practical idea in someone else.

Suggestions come from people only when they feel comfortable about presenting their ideas.

- ## Committees of Exceptionally Creative People

Because people spark ideas in others, it is important for creative people to be able to interact with each other. There are a number of ways to get creative people from different work groups together.

One way is to have people volunteer to serve on idea-evaluating committees. Such groups can evaluate a new idea, and they may be able to improve on the original suggestion. However, these committees cannot function unless there has been time and some money budgeted for their activities. Another way to encourage creative people might be to use the company bulletin board, company newspaper, or the employee-only part of the company website.

In order to be able to have a committee of creative people, you need to identify the creative people in the organization. To be able to do this, you have to recognize creative and innovative potential in work groups. The level and type of a person's creativity can sometimes be judged by how that person uses information and new ideas. Understanding this can help managers build effective teams.

Consider the material in this section and in the following space suggest ways to more effectively use the creative talents of people in your work group.

Notes:

Summary

With changes in the economy and the market, many organizations need to understand how they do business and how to modify their internal operations. How well their internal changes match these external requirements can make a significant difference in the organization's future. In a changing business environment, managers need to guide organization and not dictate the actions of all their people.

Using the ideas in this book does not require major expenditures of time or money. These ideas are what we all try to do all the time; however, here they are written to help us not forget some of the steps. The methods described are intended to serve as signposts that point the way to major changes. The book focuses on managing the decision process and the people making decisions.

These techniques are intended as a bridge from where the organization is now to where it can gain the most employee flexibility without experiencing disruptive chaos. The four special ideas can help organizations develop to where all people are responsible for promoting decisions. This book can help you create an organizational climate where those who hate change and those who love change can feel in balance. As organizations make this trip to a more flexible workplace, they can build an organizational "comfort zone" for all employees involved in decision management and in the change process.

Book Outline

Buck-Passer's Guide

Buck-Passer's Guide					
Decision Authority Levels					
Decision Considerations	Technician	Production Manager	Operations Manager	Organization Manager	Outside Authority
1. Problems					
2. Goals					
3. Action Steps					
4. Timeliness					
5. Reversibility					
6. Recoverability					
7. Impact					
8. Costs					
9. Benefits					
10. Risks					
11. Human Factors					
12. Political Factors					

This page is from the book *Change Without Chaos: A Practical Guide to Decision Management.*
Woods, David Lee (2003). Walnut Creek, CA. Summerset Books.